CASTAWAY & WRECKED

THE TIMES, WEDNESDAY,

LOSS OF THE SCHILLER.

...wing are the depositions on oath taken by the Receiver of Wreck at the Port ... pursuance of the 448th section of ... Shipping Act, 1854, which applies as well ... to English vessels that may have ... on the coasts of the United Kingdom, the ... persons examined were the mate, the ... and Mr. Henry Stern, a passenger ...

... Hillier, being duly sworn, depose as follows:— he is mate of the steamship Schiller, of ... Hamburg, of the register tonnage of 3,400 tons ... ship was owned by the Eagle Line Mail Com... of Hamburg, in the country of Germany; that the ... ship was built of iron at ... rigged as a brig, in the year 1873, and that ... classed in Lloyd's List. That the ship ... of 120 hands, including ... on board a general cargo, shipped by various ... of New York, &c., and consigned ... Germany; that the ship had on board, in addition to the ... cargo aforesaid, 254 passengers; that the ... from New York on her intended voyage on the 27th ... day of April last, at noon, the tide at the time ... being flood, the weather fine, and the wind blowing a ... moderate breeze from the south; that at the time ... of sailing the ship was in first class condition; that ... the ship was bound for Plymouth, Cherbourg, and ... Hamburg; that the ship proceeded on her intended ... voyage all well, but from the 4th to the 7th of May ... weather was hazy, with much rain; and unable to ... obtain good observations, we were steering east by ... south; that on Friday the 7th day of May, at 10 ... p.m., the tide at the time being quarter flood, the weather ... very thick, and the ship was going slowly, sails furled, steering south... rately, the ship, which, without any warning, the vessel struck. ... The engines were reversed full speed, but without avail; the ship was ... ter in order to back her off, but without avail to get the boats ... rapidly filling. Immediately this was done, but the sea was so heavy that ... out, which was done, but ... six lifeboats ...

WRECK OF AN AMERICAN LINER.

SAFETY OF THE PASSENGERS AND CREW.

Early yesterday morning the Amer... Company's Royal Mail steamship Pari... grounded on the ... dreaded Manacle rocks, near ... known as the City of Paris ... The vessel left Southampton at noon ... for New York, having on board 380 p... 572 crew, Captain Watkins being in c... weather was fine and the sea smooth ... and consequently a quick run was m... bourg, where about 60 passengers, comp... mostly steerage passengers, ... German, and Swiss peasants. At ... Saturday night the Paris left Cher... the exception that a misty rain ... down the Channel ...

THE WESTERN MORN

THE GALE IN THE WEST.

BARQUE ASHORE IN MOUNTS BAY.

RESCUE BY THE LIFEBOAT.

The boisterous weather experienced in the Three Towns on Saturday was much more severely felt to the westward and even in districts but a few miles outside Plymouth. Early on Saturday morning the attention of the people of Penzance was directed to the perilous position of the Norwegian barque Petrellen, which was riding in the bay, of 349 tons register; she was in ballast, homeward bound from Scotland. She proceeded ... up the Channel about a fortnight since as far as the Isle of ... Wight, but was then driven back to Scilly by the strong easterly ... gales that then prevailed. She eventually fetched Mount's ... Bay and anchored there for shelter. The wind having ... changed from south to south-west, the master, Captain ... Knudsen, determined on Friday afternoon to make an ... attempt to get away. Owing, however, to the strong wind ... and the heavy sea it was found impossible to beat out of ... the bay, and the Petrellen was brought up and anchored ... in the roads off St. Michael's Mount. Captain Knud-sen ... subsequently went ashore at Penzance. As the night ... advanced the weather looked very threatening and ... barometer fell rapidly, giving every indication of a dirty ... night. By many grave apprehensions were felt as to the ... safety of the barque, and more particularly wa... a fear entertained by Mr. A. Reed, the ... receiver of wreck, at whose thoughtful suggestion ... the lifeboat was brought round to the pier head as far back ... as Thursday, so that if her services should be required ... rescue might be expeditiously attempted. It was fortunate ... upon. In these events proved, that this suggestion was acte... freshened considerably, and about four a.m. blow... still gale, with heavy squalls, ... at south-south-west. ... naturally increased ... proportion as this was seen... concerning the barque, on board ... Flambeau's coastguard at Penzance ... The coastguard at Penzance ... throwing out rockets, and the lifeboat ...

Cornwall Advertiser.

MAY 15th, 1875.

The rite of confirmation was, for the ... ... living memory, administered in the ... Mylor on Friday by the Lord ... ... There were 21 candidates from ... Flushing, and although the weather ... the church was well attended. ... ... Chapel, St. Mawes.—The 11th of ... memorable day in the history of ... of this place, for on that day the ... ... boats their new chapel was laid, in the ... ber of people. The Pastor of the ... rapidly giving out the lines of Doddr... with 11 great eternal God," &c., which ... ... The Rev. Mr. Glanville, ... the Rev. Mr. ...

The WRECK of the SCHILLER.

313 LIVES LOST.

A detailed account of the dreadful catastrophe to the German steamer "Schiller," at Scilly, will be found in our second page. It was at first reported that 310 lives were lost; it is now stated that the number is 313. We here add further particulars in connexion with this shocking disaster.

Of all the tales of disasters at sea which have occurred for many years past with all their harrowing details, none can exceed in melancholy interest that of the Eagle Company steamship "Schiller." No one merely reading the particulars of similar disasters can possibly realise all or even a tithe of the truly heartrending incidents that arise. They must be seen to be understood and felt.

... steamship "Lady of the Isles," which had been ... ored, left Penzance at half-past ten o'clock ... for Scilly, taking over Mr. T. J. ... the owners of the Schiller ... underwriters, ...

THE TIMES, MONDAY, MAY 22, 1899.

SHIPWRECKS AT THE MANACLES.

(FROM A CORRESPONDENT.)

I have been at some pains to collect information as to the number of casualties that have taken place latterly within two or three miles of the Manacles. One fisherman who is still in middle life recalls 36. His list, however, is incomplete, for more than 50 have happened during the past 30 years. Of these considerably more than half may be classed as total wrecks. To turn to the lifeboat records, it seems that the Porthoustock boat, which by the three quickly ensuing wrecks, has since the year 1872 been on active service 16 times and has effected the rescue of 112 persons. The same records show that 119 lives were lost from the vessels to which the lifeboat went. There were at least 16 other wreck... that period, resulting in the ... which the lifeboat could ... some instances th... own boats. ...

When ... it may ... of advertis... adequate ... certainly c... of so little ... mentioned. ... and-a-half mil... Coastguard st... station have b... many ships from ... guard is station... to the wreck of ... increase the num... tages for them in ... out, however, that ... limited view of the ... none at all of the Ma... acquainted with the s... convinced of the emin... ing these men on Mana... there last October the ... been able to signal the N... vent her from being stran...

Next, the fact that on th... of the Mohegan the rocket... had to be laboriously pus... great hill directs attentio... able position in which the ... Save in the actual cove ... no road along the shore fro... direction. ... In full ... ... the ascent ha... ... rock...

Wreck at Scilly.

The Glasgow steamship King Cadwallon, Capt. Mowatt, 2,126 tons register, from Barry for Naples, with 5,000 tons of steam coal, struck an outlying rock off the Scillies, called Hard Lewis, during a dense fog at five o'clock on Sunday morning. Mr. Owen Legg, farmer, of St. Ellary's, heard the vessel's signals of distress, and, with his sons, put to sea in a small boat and ascertained the whereabouts of the King Cadwallon. She had her fore compartment full of water, but the crew stood by their ship. The sea was calm. In response the wired to Falmouth for a tug. The Dragon and Triton were dispatched to the scene of the wreck on Sunday morning, but were unable to render any assistance.

THE LOSS OF THE S...

LOSS OF THE SCHILLER.

Details have reached Southampton of the ... steamer Cadiz, by the arrival of the only survivor of the ... crew, George Wilson, able seaman, who has been for... warded by the British Consul at Brest. From his state... ment it appears that the loss of life is far larger than at ... first reported, 62 persons having perished. The Cadiz was ... an iron steamer of 945 tons burden, and was ... a line running between the Thames and Cadiz, belong... ing to Mr. John Hall, of London. She left Cadiz on ... the 30th of April with a cargo of wine, lead, and fruit. The ... crew consisted of 31 men, and there were 35 passengers, 20 ... of whom were Portuguese sailors coming to join a ship in ... London. The ship touched at Lisbon and Vigo, and sailed ... from the latter port for the Thames. The weather was very ... thick and foggy, and the wind was moderate, from the ... south-south-west. On Thursday night the ship struck, at ... and continued until the ship abandon... o'clock on Saturday morning on the Wyene, one of ... a number of large islands ... The captain was at the wheel. Wilson ... part of the Bay of Biscay, Mr. Atkins, was in charge of ... his cabin, the second mate, Mr. Atkins, was at the wheel. Wilson ... the watch on deck, and Wilson was not so far across ... believes the captain thought they were not so far across ... the bay as they in fact were. The captain came on deck ... as soon as the ship struck. The third mate ... forward and reported that the ship was going ... by the head. The captain ordered the six ... to be got out, but one boat ... that this could not be done. One boat ... hands, under the vessel heeling over, and ... swamped by the vessel heeling over, and three of the ... ward, drifting away with three of the ... clinging to her keel. Wilson stripped ... and swam to a rock 200 yards away ... companied him being drowned. He ... in the afternoon without food ... lifted and enabled him to see th... on another rock not far off. ... were rescued the same evenin... and lodged for the night at ... were treated with every k... taken to Brest, whence th... son to Southampton. W... than himself and the ... ribly have escaped. T... ashore is that of an E... ... way out in the ...

... As I did not think anything was the matter, I went to ... bed again and stayed there. Presently the steward ... came down and said " Get up." I told him not to ... make a noise or else he would wake my baby, and he ... replied, "If you want to wake your baby you ... had better get up." I dressed my baby and went up ... on deck. We were greatly frightened, but there was no ... confusion. They treated us very kindly, and after some ... time we were put on the tug and brought to Falmouth.

UNSUCCESSFUL ATTEMPT TO TOW OFF.

Except in the two fore compartments there was ... up to 4 o'clock yesterday afternoon no water in ... the Paris. The vessel being in an open position ... her situation is anything but satisfactory from a ... salving point of view, and a south-east wind ... means her probable destruction. At 2 o'clock ... yesterday afternoon an attempt was made to tow ... her off the rocks. Three tugs were engaged with ... ... r hawsers, and for half an hour the ... with the full pressure of steam, ... er's own engines, in vain tried to ... But she did not budge an inch, ... had eventually to be abandoned. ... ... led to Falmouth with some of ... ... cago. ...

... the Liverpool managers of the ... ... to last night stated that the ... ... g the Paris were good if the ... ... s from west or north. Pumping ... ... nished from Falmouth, Ply... ...

...ACLE ROCKS.

...ranite rocks known as the ... e and a half miles to the ... ... bour, and near it are the ... ... wine, and Vaze. The ... scene of many mari... ... which the monu... ... St. Keverne parish ... It is usual for trans... ... or 15 miles to the ... ... it was through the ... ring a course that ... ... the northward of the ... ... he coastline where ... ... rocks are par... ... the sea, can ... ... exposed by the ... ... southern ex... ... bour, and it ... ... that the safe ... lights of St. ... Harbour ... ... ard, but it ... ... ore might ... warning ... ... ous spot. ... ... anacles. ... ... gard the ... ... ning of ... ... m the ... ... rock...

AN AUSTRIAN BARQUE ASHORE AT PORTHLEVEN.

LOSS OF THREE LIVES.

DARING RESCUE.

[FROM OUR OWN REPORTER.]

Once more the eastern side of Mount's Bay has been the scene of a disastrous shipwreck, attended with loss of life, the result of the severe gale of Saturday last. From early morning Porthleven coastguard had been keeping a careful look-out seaward on the chance of any vessel needing assistance, and this watch was the more anxiously kept from the fact that the wind, which had veered from west to west-south-west, was one which usually causes disasters in this neighbourhood. All day the wind raged furiously, and a cold, penetrating rain, while it obscured the view, almost blinded those who attempted to face it. The sea was running mountains high, washing over the face of the high cliffs with which Porthleven is surrounded, and rolling huge boulders one over the other like marbles. At four o'clock, when the tide was at its height and the wind blowing its hardest, the watch on shore descried a large ship to the south-south-west, coming directly toward the land under lower foretopsail, foretopmast-staysail, and mizen staysail. It was at once seen that the ship was in imminent danger, from the fact of her main-topsail having been carried away, and that she was embayed without any possible means of weathering the Lizard; while the state of the sea prevented any possibility of anchoring. All efforts were, therefore, immediately directed towards endeavour-ing to guide the ill-fated vessel towards the most suit-able position for running her ashore, and for pre-paring to rescue the crew. Towards attaining the first object a white flag was waved from the topmost scaffolding of the new library which Mr. W. Bickford-Smith is erecting near the foot of the southern pier; while, at the same time, the coast-guard-men promptly got the rocket-apparatus out and brought it down to the cliff about two hundred yards south of the pier, where by this time (4.15 p.m.) it could be seen the vessel must strike. The news spread like wildfire through the village and, within seven minutes from the time the was first observed, the rocket-apparatus was ... spot, ready for use, and the cliff thronged ... hundreds of anxious and eager spectators. ... life-saving gear was under the superintenden... chief officer Beckerleg, who had with him an ... crew, consisting of chief-boatman John H ... Jenkin, and boatmen C. Mahoney and W. ... commissioned-boatmen W. Mahoney and W. ...

At the same time coxswain and secretary ... Mr. Symons, harbour-master and secretary ... lifeboat-committee, made everything ready f... launching of the lifeboat, in case she was neede... less time than it takes to write these wor... barque bounded on towards her doom, th... washing over her, and the crew being clea... clinging to the rigging, having apparen... hope of attempting to do min... hope which was unh... far as th...

The Penzance Gazette.

WEDNESDAY, JANUARY 13, 1841.

DREADFUL SHIPWRECK OF THE THAMES STEAMER— 61 LIVES LOST.

The Packet-boat Lord Wellington, Tre... berthan, master, which arrived here on Friday last from Scilly, brought most harrowing intelligence of the total wreck of the Thames Steamer, on her passage from Dublin to Fal-mouth, and the loss of sixty one persons, out of 66 who were on board!

This ill-fated vessel left Dublin on Saturday, the 2nd instant, bound to London, to touch, as usual, at Falmouth and Plymouth; and the fatal catastrophe which we have now the painful task to relate, occurred on the following Monda... 5 o'clock in the morning, at which time ... ... w a very heavy gale, had driven the ves... ... rather Westward than her proper course, ... at owing to the fall of Snow here pre... ... tion was not known. A light con... ... inly through the falling Snow, & the Cap... ... nd Mate were not agreed in opinion as to ... ... ight it was— the former believing it to b... ... longships, (a short distance from the La... ... nd,) and the latter, the St. Agnes lig... ... Scilly,) while this question was under disc... ... the vessel shipped a sea which extinguis... ... fires and of course stopped the engine... ... command over her being now lost, she ... ... mercy of the elements, and effo... ... set sail upon her, but before ... ... her under direc... ...'s Rock...

Castaway & Wrecked

REX COWAN

Duckworth

Suave, mari magno turbantibus aequora ventis,
e terra magnum alterius spectare laborem;
non quia vexari quemquamst iucunda voluptas,
sed quibus ipse malis careas quia cernere suave est.

Lucretius 2.1-4

When storms rage over the ocean, it is good to
stand on shore and observe others in distress – not
because there is any joy or pleasure to be had in
other people's troubles, but because it is good to
see from what misfortunes you are free yourself.

tr. Colin Haycraft

First published in 1978 by
Gerald Duckworth & Co. Ltd
The Old Piano Factory
43 Gloucester Crescent, London NW1

New text and editorial arrangement © 1978 by Rex Cowan
Photographs © 1978 by Frank Gibson

cased ISBN 0 7156 1145 3
paper ISBN 0 7156 1146 1

Printed by B A S Printers Ltd
Over Wallop, Hampshire.

Contents

THE GIBSONS

JOHN GIBSON (1827–1920)
died in St. Buryan, Cornwall

ALEXANDER GENDALL
GIBSON
(1857–1944)
buried in Oswestry

HERBERT JOHN
GIBSON
(1861–1937)
died in Scilly

JAMES GIBSON
(1900–   )
lives in Penzance

FRANCIS (Frank)
GIBSON
(1929–   )
lives and practises in Scilly

Introduction

A shipwreck is a battle between man and nature, and as a battle it has its heroes, its cowards, its incompetents and its victims. This book is a marriage between written and photographic reportage. The prose, mainly of Victorian journalists, is presented alongside photographs taken by the Gibson family of Scilly and Penzance whose near-fanatical obsession with shipwrecks at the time produced a series of visual images of such power, insight and nostalgia that even the most passive observer cannot fail to feel the excitement or pathos of the events that they depict.

In the nineteenth century newspaper reporters and photographers worked independently, and sometimes with different aims. It is hard to realise that, though photographic techniques improved rapidly from about 1850, it was not possible to reproduce a photograph speedily in newsprint until the beginning of the twentieth century, although in the later years of the nineteenth century, with more time for preparation, and a different quality of paper, weekly illustrated journals like *The Illustrated London News* did supplement their engraved drawings of events with news and features illustrated with photographs. The 'terrible scenes' of the wreck of the *Mohegan* in 1898 were reported with agonising detail in the newspapers within a day or two of the occurrence, and Alexander Gibson was there with his camera to record much of it. But it was not until 22 October, eight days after the wreck, that *The Illustrated London News* carried a feature with words and pictures; with all the technical problems and delays in communication, that was good going for those days. It is in the magazine's edition of 21 December 1907 that the combination of Gibson photographs and news reporting is first seen – a rare and previously forgotten example researched from the newspaper archives. The photographs are not in the present Gibson collection, and it is not known where the negatives are, if indeed they have survived.

By juxtaposing the contemporary newspaper accounts with the wreck photographs, I try in this book to show how they can complement and supplement each other. Modern journalism, which has to combine text and photographs simultaneously, with the needs of speed and brevity taking precedence, has tended to make shipwrecks (and other subjects) duller and less dramatic. Early editions of the *Daily Mirror* and *Daily Graphic,* the first tabloids, published at the beginning of the century, carry less text, are more vulgarly written and frequently use photographs taken by staff photographers.

Without the aid of photographs or drawings, the early reporter *had* to find evocative words to convey the flavour of his story. It is not just sentimentality for the phraseology of the past that makes the accounts presented in this book so attractive, but the elegance of the phrases and the intrinsic excellence of the storytelling: for instance, the following description of the scene at the dread Manacles Rocks where the *Mohegan* was sunk:

> Jutting out from the mainland topped by the spire of St. Keverne Church, is a beetling chain of treacherous rocks – treacherous, sharp, insidious. When weather is fair and light is clear, no mariner needs run his craft into the jaws of death which here may await him, for at all states of the tide one or more of the treacherous fangs rise gaunt and steep out of the waves.

Or almost a hundred years earlier in *The Times* the description of the *Anson* drownings:

> At a time when no one appeared on the ship's deck, and it was supposed the work of death had ceased...

The Gibsons, arriving with their cameras as soon as possible, saw truly that the story to be told in their photographs was not just the immediate catastrophe and crisis of the wreck, but also the aftermath. They were as concerned with the burials, inquests, rescue attempts, salvage of cargo and ship's furniture, and the subsequent diving (sometimes included where it hadn't been possible to photograph the actual wreck, as with the *Anson* and the *Zelda*), as well as with the human feelings of the actors and onlookers.

It is easy to speculate, as art historians do with painters, about the motives and ideas of the photographers as they clicked their shutters. They have left us little to go on. John, Alexander and Herbert Gibson were not communicative men – not, anyway, about the driving forces behind their appetite for shipwreck. But some conclusions can be drawn from the photographic evidence. With what dashing cheek, for instance, did Alexander induce the 'young lad' Willis, one of the three survivors of the 'Terrible Shipping Calamity' of the *Khyber,* picked up near to death from some wreckage on the beach, to pose later in his studio after that frightening experience, against a painted background of rocks and sea!

Some of the photographs form a series, each one telling a part of the story, or emphasising some particular point. The *Khyber* was smashed to pieces in ten minutes. Cheated by the storm of that scene on his film, Alexander painted it, and photographed the painting. He photographed from the top of

the cliff the matchwood debris, all that was left of the 2,000-ton ship, with clusters of curious onlookers picking through the wreckage, which looks like an accumulation of flotsam. Then, coming down to the cove, he took a close-up of the masts and – so that we should know that it was once a brave ship – put the figurehead in the foreground. The verbal account in *The Royal Cornwall Gazette* two days later complements Alexander's photographs with an uncanny fidelity. It would be hard to find a better example of these two ways of telling a story: both full of meaning, feeling and information, yet with an economy of detail that sharpens the impact on the reader and viewer. Not all wreck stories are exciting or dramatic. Herbert artfully combines his picture of the re-building of Bishop Rock Lighthouse with the view of the masts and hull of the *Castleford,* stuck fast on the rocky islet of Crebawethen, which a sharp eye can pick out in the distant background. The ship nuzzles forlornly against the rock, on which the black cattle stand or lie in their mournful safety – a focus of interest in this tedious and uneventful wreck.

Alexander and Herbert had no need to earn a living from ship photographs; the portrait business in and around Penzance was a lucrative and thriving one, and they had a large slice of it. It was something else that brought Alexander and his hundredweight of equipment back several times to Porthleven to photograph the *Cviet* in each stage of her condition, as she lay stranded and beached, and was broken up: something beyond mere interest. Perhaps he was stimulated by the courage of her Captain, or by the 'noble conduct' of the Porthleven fishermen, and returned to the scene to catch the final atmosphere of the 'fatal wreck'. The 'boiling surf' had done its job by the time Alexander or Herbert (attributions are often doubtful) got to the *Seine*.

One theme continually occurs, both in the news accounts and in the photographs – death. This is not perhaps surprising, since death is the almost inevitable accompaniment of a violent shipwreck. In the news accounts death is repeatedly linked with heroism – another recurrent theme. Death and injury always invite curiosity; witness the eager onlookers today at a car accident or airline crash, the modern forms of transportation disaster. But there the parallel ends. Car accidents are often the result of negligence or culpable error and tend to involve no heroic acts. In Victorian and Edwardian shipwreck stories, on the other hand, there are frequent allusions to heroism, which invest the deaths with dignity. Even allowing for such different expectations of heroic behaviour as existed at the time, the frequency of brave acts by sailor and rescuer is remarkable. It is paralleled by the valour of lifeboat and helicopter rescue crews today, which stands out starkly in an anti-heroic anti-romantic age.

The wreck of the *Cviet* with foreigners aboard gave a simple Cornish fisherman, Joseph Gilbert, his moment of modest bravery:

> Much has been said in favour of the noble conduct . . . of Joseph Gilbert, who successfully threw the line on board, thus being the means of saving eight of the crew. At times when he was going toward the ship, the waves took him off his legs and for nearly a minute he would disappear beneath the seething waters, so that at times the bystanders thought he would be drowned.

On the stricken *Mohegan,* 'the crew behaved like heroes. The Captain stood on the bridge and the greatest order prevailed among officers and crew', and in the midst of a 'scene of the wildest excitement' the 'boy' Henry Oldridge from the *G. I. Jones* was rescued by a 'number of women who waded out into the water' when he had been washed on to a rock. These events could be recorded and reproduced by the reporter, but less easily by the camera, except symbolically. On the spot with the speed and sophistication of a modern television crew, Alexander (or was it Herbert?) captured the brave skill of the Sennen Rocket life-saving brigade, perched on the steep cliffs of Mill Bay, as he photographed the hair-raising, high-wire journey of the crew of the sinking *City of Cardiff*.

But it is in the portrayal of death that the Gibsons' cameras are most subtle. While the writer personifies the sea in words – the cruel sea, the fickle sea – its victims are arraigned in person by the camera. They are the losers in the battle; so what happens to them afterwards is an important ceremony. They remind us of our own mortality; and partly because we feel some shame at our relief at not being dead ourselves, we desire to see their bodies treated with care and respect. We take fright at dismemberment but sometimes can't stop looking at it or reading about it. In one account (not included here) of the *Khyber,* there are lengthy descriptions of the gruesome remains of the crew: portions of hands and feet, 'the outside covering of a head lying flat with the features, including a moustache, intact, but the ears gone'. The remains were carefully collected for the Coroner, having been washed and diligently looked after for burial by the Rev. Trimmer Bennett.

The Gibsons compel us to look at the rituals, and they show

us what our ancestors felt. After the wreck of the *Mohegan* in which one hundred and six people died, a cart carries the body of a girl victim in the straw. Alexander fixes the faces of the onlookers clustered round, curious, anxious, nervous, thoughtful and straining shyly to see the corpse – not one without a hat or cap: then the newly-made coffins, safe and quiet in the haven of the (heated) church, and finally, in a mass grave, the sombre diggers, bareheaded. The camera seems to give a momentary relief by catching the attention of all the mourners – except for the one with his hands in his pockets, eyes fixed on the coffins. Laid out for identification on pieces of wooden wreckage, with sad white feet bare like their faces, members of the crew of the *G. I. Jones* are spared by death from witnessing the pompous formality of the Penzance Coroner's inquest. Though the photographer missed the ship-wreck itself, he provides us with a piece of social history from its aftermath.

Frequently the photographs anticipate the newspaper story, for John Gibson was a superb photo-journalist. He was the first telegraphist when the telegraph was installed in Scilly and had an instinctive understanding of what would make good news. Many of the dramatic stories published round the world after the wreck of the *Schiller* on Retarriers Reef were composed by him. Alexander, an apt pupil, was often at his side as he tapped out his messages. Shipwreck stories were their diet.

Everywhere in these photographs there is acute observation, attention to detail, concentration on sub-plots, posed fillers to give balance and composition, artfulness in touching up skies and slowing down waves too fast for the camera's exposures. Never content with one perspective, the Gibsons would take several films from different angles. The first of the *Suffolk* photographs, for instance, shows the view taken off her starboard side after she broke her back on the Lizard. From another view, her bows on the rocks, the frightened cattle huddled on her forepeak wait for rescue – which didn't come for the ones whose carcases were photographed being dragged up the cliff path by horse and cart. Approaching the *Malta,* a hybrid steamship with steadying sails, the photographer was able to take not only the details of her name on the bow but her incongruous female figurehead, neither of which were visible from the other view.

Here, then, in this book are two art forms, words and pictures, together for the first time – a conjunction that their authors never expected. I have chosen the best and most

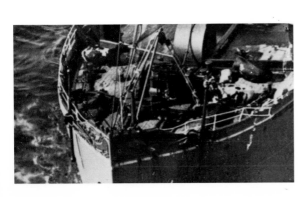

descriptive of the many newspaper accounts that exist for each wreck, and I reproduce them as they were originally published, edited in some cases when too long. Where possible I have captioned the photographs with extracts from the newspaper copy. If no Gibson is named it is because I cannot attribute the photograph with confidence. Many of the photographs have never been published in this form before.

Frank Gibson, the remaining Gibson practitioner, survives and thrives, still photographing shipwrecks for himself and the newspapers, as intrepid as his forebears. While this book was being compiled he was precariously hovering near the Bishop Rock Lighthouse in a small low-flying aircraft, near to the speed of stall, photographing a modern scene – the relief of the Light by helicopter from a pad built on the tower. This is not a shipwreck, but it is the same sort of story, and I include the photograph here unashamedly.

'Castaway & wrecked' is an expression which has come down from the sixteenth century. It implies that the sea has a will. If, as I have postulated, a shipwreck reminds us of our own mortality, then these words and pictures now joined together deserve a small place in immortality.

Acknowledgments

My thanks are due to Frank Gibson of Scilly who generously opened his extensive collection of negative plates, and not only allowed me free rein to collect some of the finest photographs, but also patiently answered my frequent enquiries and prepared fine prints of the selected photographs for publication. I am also grateful to the helpful and efficient staff of the British Library's newspaper collection at Colindale. The Library kindly granted permission for the reproduction of the extracts used in this book. Dick Larn readily filled in some unknown facts for me from his encyclopedic knowledge of Victorian Cornish shipwrecks, and my wife Zélide Cowan, who first fully appreciated the importance and attraction of the Gibson shipwreck photographs, supported my venture throughout. An anonymous hand kindly supplied missing commas and expunged superfluous ones. The back cover photograph is by Frank Gibson and depicts his grandfather's whole-plate camera against the sea at Scilly.

H.M.S. Anson

' By three o'clock, no appearance of the vessel remained. She was an old ship (a 64, we believe, cut down), which accounts for her beating to pieces on a sandy bottom.'

The Times, December 29, 1807

ANSON FRIGATE.

The following further particulars of the melancholy loss of this ship are given chiefly on the authority of the officers who were saved:—The *Anson* sailed from Falmouth on Christmas-eve, for her station off the Black Rocks, as one of the look-out frigates of the Channel Fleet. In the violent storm of Monday, blowing about W. to S. W. she stood across the entrance of the Channel, towards Scilly, made the Land's End, *which they mistook for The Lizard,* and bore up, as they

'At a time when no one appeared on the ship's deck and it was supposed the work of death had ceased, a Methodist Preacher, venturing his life through the surf, got on board, over the wreck of the main-mast, to see if any more remained.'

thought for Falmouth. Still doubtful, however, in the evening of Monday, Captain LYDIARD stood off again to the southward; when a consultation being held, it was once more resolved to bear up for Falmouth.— Running eastward and northward, still under the fatal persuasion that the *Lizard* was on the north-west of them, they did not discover the mistake till the man on the look-out a-head, called out "breakers!"— The ship was instantaneously broached-to, and the bower let go, which happily brought her up: but the rapidity with which the cable had veered out, made it impossible to serve it, and it soon parted in the hawse-hole. The sheet anchor was then let go, which also brought up the ship; but after riding end-on for a short time, this cable parted from the same cause, about eight in the morning, and the ship went plump on shore, upon the ridge of sand which separates the Loe-pool from the bay. Never did the sea run more tremendously high. It broke over the ship's masts, which soon went by the board; the main-mast forming a floating raft from the ship to the shore; and the greater part of those who escaped, passed by this medium. One of the men saved reports, that Captain LYDIARD was near him on the main-mast; but he seemed to have lost the use of his faculties, with horror of the scene, and soon disappeared. We have not room to go farther into particulars, nor language that will convey an adequate picture of the terrific view that presented itself; but justice demands the relation of the following anecdote.

At a time when no one appeared on the ship's deck, and it was supposed the work of death had ceased, a Methodist Preacher, venturing his life through the surf, got on board, over the wreck of the main-mast, to see if any more remained—some honest hearts followed him. They found several persons still below, who could not get up; among whom were two women and two children. The worthy Preacher and his party saved the two women and some of the men; but the children were irretrievably lost. About two P.M. the ship went to pieces; when a few more men, *who for some crime had been confined in irons below*, emerged from the wreck; one of these was saved. By three o'clock, no appearance of the vessel remained. She was an old ship (a 64, we believe, cut down), which accounts for her beating to pieces so soon on a sandy bottom.

The men who survived, were conveyed to Helston, about two miles distant, where they were taken care of by the Magistrates, and afterwards sent to Falmouth in charge of the Regulating Captain at that port. We are aware that general report has stated the number drowned to be greater than we have given it; but of the missing, we understand many are deserters, who scampered off as soon as they reached the shore. Among the officers saved, we have heard of the following:—Captain SULLIVAN, a passenger; Messrs. HILL and BRAILY, Midshipmen; Mr. ROSS, Assistant Surgeon, and some others.

Too early for the invention of photography, and therefore for the Gibsons, *H.M.S. Anson*, a frigate of 64 guns on Channel Patrol, went aground in the breakers near Looe in 1807, as a result of faulty navigation. In 1912, ever watchful, Alexander photographed the old 'hard hat' divers working for the Western Marine Salvage Co. Ltd., when they recovered a large cannon and other objects. Jubilant and dressed in their Sunday best, Captain Anderson and his wife, children and salty crew were posed in the hold of the salvage vessel by Alexander. A group of onlookers can be seen in these photographs, evidence of how close to the shore the ship struck – near enough for the Methodist preacher to wade out. The cannon is now buried vertically in the ground at Porthleven shipyard, its muzzle serving as a bollard.

The Thames

Falmouth Packet and Cornish Herald, January 16, 1841

DREADFUL SHIPWRECK.
Loss of the Thames Steamer on the Scilly Rocks.

In our last publication we announced the appalling event of the wreck of the *Thames* steamer, and the loss of sixty-one human beings, and the whole of the valuable cargo.

From the evidence of the survivors, taken before the coroner and a respectable jury on the 6th inst., to inquire into the death of the bodies then found, it appears that the Thames, commanded by Capt. Grey, left Dublin on Saturday the 2nd inst., for Plymouth and London; during her passage was driven a great way out of her course, and when she made the Scilly light mistook it for the Long-ship light at the Land's End. The seaman saved says the Light was in sight when he came on deck at 4 a.m., (of Monday the 4th instant,) but how long the light had been seen previous he could not say, and that the other sailors said it was the Long-ship's light, but about half an hour after she shipped a sea that filled her, and stopped the engines; they then discovered the rocks around them, and that it must be Scilly. The captain had sail put on her, but the ship became unmanageable, and about five o'clock struck on some rocks near an uninhabited island called Rosevere. A boat from St. Agnes, the nearest inhabited island, went to the ship, at imminent risk, and succeeded in taking off the wreck a Miss Morris, one of the passengers, and the two stewardesses: the boat dared not near the ship, fearing a rush from those on board; they had, therefore, to draw the females through the sea by a rope fastened round the waist, one end on board the ship—the other end the boatman had. This was about halfpast eight o'clock a.m., and shortly after a very heavy hail storm came on, when all hopes vanished of having any more assistance from shore; the flood set in, and the wind increased to a heavy gale, with very severe hail storms from N.E. to E.N.E. The boat which had the survivors on board, and another boat attempting to make the ship, were nearly lost: the former was not found till some hours after by a large pilot boat, when the people were taken on board and the boat towed into St. Agnes; the scene of the wreck is about 3 miles to the N.W. of that island. The ship had only two boats; one was stove in by a sea, the other some recruits got into, and lowered her into the water before any on board were aware of it; two gentlemen jumped for her, but jumped short, sank, and were seen no more; the recruits not being able to manage the boat, she soon filled, went down, and they also soon perished. Thus were sixty or seventy human creatures left without any means of saving themselves, and in such a dangerous place, three miles from any inhabited island, and, after nine o'clock, a.m. no hope whatever of any assistance from the shore. The seaman saved states that about ten a.m. the quarter-deck began to give way, (all under water forward,) when the captain with about twenty more got into the main rigging. They were not long there before the main-mast went overboard, and all soon perished, either by drowning, or killed by the fall. At this time there were many more on the quarter-deck, when about eleven o'clock it was lifted up in a body by the sea, and afterwards separated into several pieces, on one of which this sailor stood with seven more fellow creatures; four only besides himself reached the island, Rosevere, (a short distance from the wreck,) the others were washed off whilst floating between the wreck and the shore; when the raft reached the shore, they were all washed off by a heavy sea: the man saved fortunately got hold of a rock, held till the sea receded, and then scrambled a little higher up till he found he was safe; he then looked round for the others, but never saw them. He soon began to look for shelter for the night, when shortly he found a porter barrel; he knocked in the head, and crept into it, otherwise he would likely have perished of cold, the night (Monday) was very severe. Next morning, by break of day, he was taken off, as were also the dead bodies of seven men and one woman. The stewardess recognised the bodies of Jack, (the steward), a seaman, Griffiths, a stoker, name unknown, another seaman, named Quin, or Quinlan, belonged to Dublin; another seaman, name unknown, and one recruit. The female was the wife of a soldier, who also perished, as did also the little infant which the mother was suckling. The names of those saved are a Miss Morris, whose father perished on board, a Mrs. Myers, first-cabin stewardess, Mary Gregory, second cabin stewardess, and J. Kearnes, seaman. Unfortunately for this shipwreck, all the large pilotboats were high and dry when they would have been of vast service; for, had they been afloat, they, early in the morning—say from seven till nine o'clock—in all likelihood would have saved every soul, as they are large enough, and could have received the passengers and crew from the smaller boats as they took them from the ship, but this could not have been done later than half past eight or nine o'clock. It has been a most heartrending shipwreck. The frantic cries of the sufferers could be heard occasionally at St. Agnes.

The Times, January 14, 1841

The following is the copy of a letter from one of the stewardesses of the Thames, to her father and mother: "Scilly Light-house, Island of St. Agnes. My dear father and mother,—God in his mercy has spared me and Mary Gregory, and one more young lady, the name of Miss Morris; any more belonging to the boat I can give no account of at present. I tremble to write, and be obliged to say the Thames is gone to pieces at the above island. Captain Grey saved our lives, and, what shall I say! must I say! he is gone, he may be alive, but if he is, he must be on the rocks, and if it be pleasing to my good God, may he be spared. May he be spared to his family; his praise is

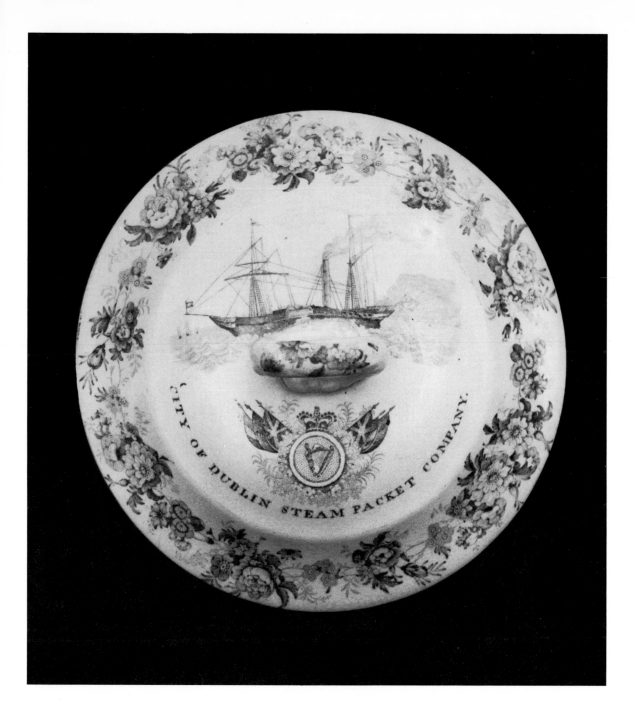

beyond my pen, to say that he saved our lives by throwing a rope around us, and then we jumped into the sea; the life-boat picked us up, and as far as our state will allow we are receiving every kindness. My dear father and mother, I am able to write very little; I shall write a few lines to my children. Call at the office, tell one of the young gentlemen you heard from me. The packet struck at 6 o'clock in the morning, and went to pieces at 10. I hope in my good God I shall have better news in the morning; if I have, I will write directly again. The storm is so severe here, the boat cannot venture out. Pray for Captain Grey. I can say no more. I remain, &c., MARY MEYLER."

'Captain Grey saved our lives, and what shall I say – must I say! He is gone, he may be alive, but if he is, he must be on the rocks, and if it be pleasing to my good God, may he be spared . . . Pray for Captain Grey. I can say no more.'

In 1841 the Steam Packet *Thames* sank within four hours of striking an awesome reef, the 'Brow of Ponds', on the outer fringes of the Scillies, and immediately broke to pieces. Following tradition, Frank Gibson photographed the china lid of a pot from the wreck site illustrating the vessel, which was recovered by divers exploring the area in 1973.

The **Minnehaha**

'A scene of terrible confusion ensued . . . The chief mate and other survivors scrambled, although in imminent peril, from the mizzen to the mainmast, thence on to the foremast, dropping down the bowsprit stays.'

Lake's Falmouth Packet and Cornwall Advertiser

January 24, 1874

Wreck of a Ship at Scilly.
LOSS OF TEN LIVES.

A fatal shipwreck occurred early on Sunday morning at Peninnis Head, the Southernmost point of St. Mary's, Scilly. Between two and three o'clock on Sunday morning there was a heavy sea falling on all the western parts of the Islands. The ship "Minnehaha," of Liverpool, of 845 tons register, owned by Messrs. Hughes, of Menai Bridge, Holyhead, and commanded by Captain Jones, arrived at Falmouth a short time since from Guanape with a cargo of guano. She received orders for Dublin, and left for that place on Friday afternoon, having on board a channel pilot named Volk. At three o'clock on Sunday morning St. Agnes light was made, but very indistinctly, owing to the thickness of the weather. At this time the ship was standing to the N.W., under easy canvas, when she suddenly struck on a rock with great violence. It would appear that the port bow was stove right in, for the water poured into the vessel a perfect deluge, and within two minutes she was almost under water. A scene of terrible confusion ensued, and those of the crew who had not been overwhelmed rushed into the tops. Among them was Capt. Jones, who reached the mizen top in safety, and who determined to swim ashore for assistance. He took off his clothes for this purpose, but through some cause, probably by becoming chilled, relaxed his hold and fell into the sea, and nothing more was seen or heard of him. The chief mate and other survivors scrambled, although in imminent peril, from the mizen to the mainmast, thence on to the foremast, dropping down the bowsprit stays. By this time the vessel had so far settled down that the water was level with the topgallant forecastle deck, and it was with the greatest difficulty that they managed to reach the rocks, and thence got ashore. They then discovered that besides Captain Jones and Mr. Volk eight of the crew were also drowned, the survivors being Robert Thomas (chief mate), Martin Petterson, Thomas Childs, John Small, William Waters, Robert Owen Noils, Christen Sarowson, John Williams, and William Bremer. The ship and cargo will be a total loss. The "Minnehaha" was built at St. John's, New Brunswick, in 1857.

Another account says:—The weather was very thick at the time, with rain. St. Agnes light was seen a little before the ship struck, but it was supposed to be the Wolf, and that the ship was going safely between the Wolf and the Land's End. When the light was seen they were about to heave-to for soundings, but then orders were given to keep away, hoping to go between the Scilly Isles and the Wolf. The coast where the ship was wrecked is a bold point, having 20 fathoms of water close to the shore. The master, (Captain Jones), the pilot, second mate, carpenter, sailmaker, and five sailors were drowned; including the pilot there were 20 on board. The pilot's name was Volk, of Glyn Cottage, Falmouth. The ten men who were saved got up over the rocks and went in search of houses. They got to a barn belonging to Mr. Thomas Bluett, and asked his workman to give them a few turnips as they were hungry and cold. They were then taken into the town to the Telegraph Hotel, and Mr. Burton, the agent of the Shipwrecked Fishermen and Mariners' Society, supplied them with clothing. Salvors were employed to save the sails, rigging, boats, &c. The ship was uninsured; she had been 14 months on the voyage from Peru with guano. Had the crew all got into the rigging, and waited till daylight, they would all have been saved; but, as is frequently the case, in the great alarm efforts were made to get ashore, and not seeing where they were going, it leads to fatal accidents. When the masts stand, it is much safer to remain by the ship until daylight. The cargo is all lost, and the ship is fast breaking up. This is the first shipwreck, attended with loss of life, which has occurred on St. Mary's Island within the memory of man.

The Zelda

Lake's Falmouth Packet and Cornwall Advertiser,
April 18, 1874

Wreck at Scilly.—On Thursday soon after midnight during a dense fog the protracted scream of a steam whistle was heard at Bryher, and a gig's crew went off from the place, and found that the new steamer "Zelda", Pierce, master, thirteen hundred tons register, belonging to Messrs. Glynn, and of and from Liverpool for Palermo, laden with rice, iron, and sundries, had struck on Maiden Bower, the north-westernmost Isle of Scilly, and sunk almost immediately. This was the ship's first voyage. The crew, thirty-two in number, and two passengers were saved in the boats, but lost all their effects. The ship has broken in two, her bows are in ten fathoms, and the stern in five fathoms at low water.

Another wreck which sank too quickly and eluded the photographer was the *Zelda*, 1300 tons, laden with rice and iron. The divers came shortly afterwards to salvage her cargo, and Herbert took another 'aftermath' picture of the diving operations.

The Tabasco

Never to be frustrated, Alexander, the most
eccentric of the Gibsons, and a talented if quirky
water-colourist, painted this highly imaginative
surrealistic representation of the wreck of the
Tabasco, a 215-ton Bordeaux Barquentine, laden
with a welcome cargo of coal and bottled beer,
which went down off White Island, Scilly, on
24 March 1879. He then photographed his
painting and sold postcard reproductions.

The G. I. Jones

Lake's Falmouth Packet and Cornwall Advertiser

September 8, 1883

THE GREAT GALE.

During the height of the storm, the barque, G. I. Jones, of Newport, Monmouth, from Bull River, with a cargo of phosphate, Captain W. Norton, went ashore at Cuddan Point, in Mount's Bay. The coastguard-men with rocket apparatus were soon in attendance, but the night was so dark that for a long time nothing could be seen of the barque. At length, between ten and eleven o'clock, cries of distress were heard above the roaring of the gale, and guided by these the rocket apparatus was manned on the cliff above Men Dhu Cove, inside Cuddan Point. By the light of the rockets the barque could be made out. She was lying broadside on, with a heavy list towards the land, and with all three masts standing. The crew were seen huddled together in the forerigging, and the sea was making clean breaches over the hull. Nearly a dozen rockets were fired, and three at least fell across the vessel. But the crew, either exhausted or paralysed by fear, or unable to reach either of the lines, made no attempt to haul the hawser on board. It was only when the rockets were being fired that the barque could be seen; but when the vessel was hidden from view the noise of her smashing on the rocks could distinctly be heard. At length a boy and man were seen washing ashore, and willing hands going out into the surf soon secured them. These two were the only survivors out of the crew of thirteen hands, and in addition there was a St. Mawes pilot Mr. James Andrew, on board, so that twelve souls had gone into eternity within a short space of time.

From the statement of the survivors it would seem that prior to the vessel going ashore, every man was on deck. The pilot thought to weather the Lizard, but this was found to be impossible. The pilot then told the captain that he did not think the vessel could get out of the bay, and they had better try to get to Penzance to save both vessel and crew. The ship got round one point, but could not weather the next (the Grebe), so it was determined to put out two anchors. The starboard and port anchors were accordingly let go, with eighty fathoms of chain, but neither anchor acted, and the ship gradually drove on to the shore on a mass of rocks. From this point it was a case of every man for himself, and all had to hold on for dear life, as the sea instantly commenced to sweep the vessel. Prior to the vessel breaking up the pilot was in the deck-house, which was almost full of water. He stood there some time up to his neck in water, and at last said, "God help me; I am done for now." He fell into the water, and the efforts of two of the crew to get him out were unavailing. The captain was on the poop, the rest of the crew being in the foremast rigging, excepting the second mate, the carpenter, and the cook; these latter, with the two survivors and the other boy, were all together. They could hear the men forward shrieking, but their cries ceased about fifteen minutes before the masts were carried away and no doubt they were washed away from the rigging. At last with a fearful crash the masts gave way and the vessel broke up. Henry Oldridge, one of the two saved, is a boy. He was washed on to a rock, and was rescued by a number of women, who waded out into the water, amid a scene of the wildest excitement.

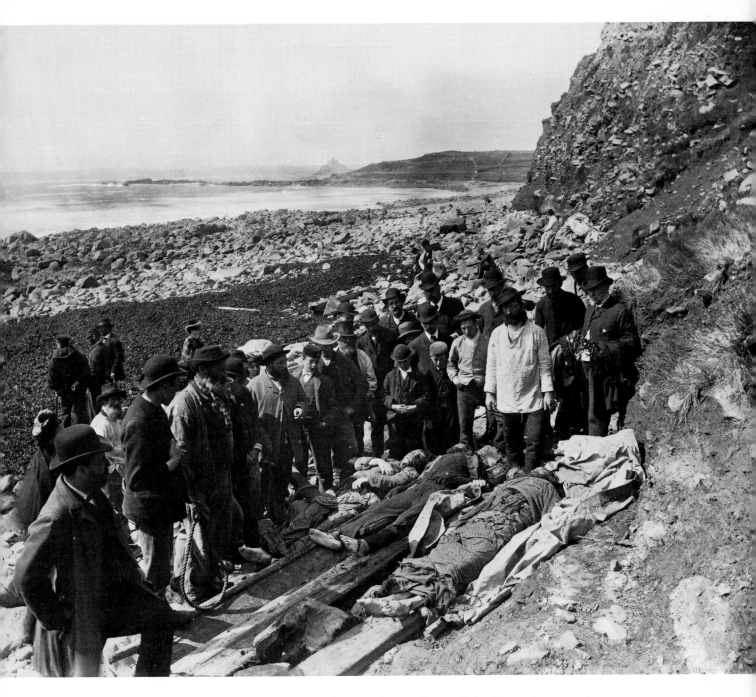

'. . . so that twelve souls had gone into eternity
within a short space of time.' '. . . God Help
me! I am done for now.'

The Cviet

Western Morning News, January 30, 1884

THE FATAL WRECK AT PORTHLEVEN.

An inquest was held at the Commercial Hotel, Porthleven, on Monday afternoon, by Mr. P. G. Grenfell, county coroner, touching the death of Mattea Roccovich, 37, one of the crew of the Austrian barque Cviet, which was wrecked on Porthleven beach on Saturday afternoon. Mr. John Simons, harbourmaster, was foreman of the jury. Giovanni Miletich, deposed that he was the mate of the Cviet. They last sailed from St. Domingo with a cargo of logwood, and were bound to Falmouth for orders. All went well until they sighted the Scilly Isles, at five o'clock on Friday afternoon. They had then been out 46 days. A great storm came on from the south-west, driving the vessel before it. At eleven o'clock Saturday morning the maintopsail was blown away. They were then 4 or 5 miles west of the Lizard, and lying to, and gradually drifting into Mount's Bay. The ship was then put about, standing away from the Lizard. At three in the afternoon all hands gave up hope of saving the vessel. The witness had just before seen land in front and behind them. A short time afterwards she struck on the sand. The sea swept over the deck and broke the bulwarks. All hands took to the rigging for safety. The captain, Guiseppe Matcovich, was above witness in the fore rigging. Two or three big seas struck the fore part of the ship, knocking the captain overboard, and he was seen no more. The deceased, Roccovich, lowered himself with a rope over the side of the ship nearest to the shore, and, after struggling in the waves for a minute or two, he sank. The ship was a good one, and was well found in everything. The witness had no complaint either against the captain or any of the crew. They all did their best to save the vessel. The mate could speak English sufficiently well to give his evidence without the aid of an interpreter.—Thomas Laity, a fisherman of Porthleven, deposed that on Sunday morning, a little after seven, he found the body of the deceased on the beach about 300 yards from the Looe Bar. He had on only his trousers. The body was taken to the lifeboat house, Porthleven. The face and head were much bruised. Witness was present when the Cviet went ashore, and assisted in saving part of the crew. No more could be done than was done on that occasion. There was a lifeboat at Porthleven, but the weather was too bad to put it out on Saturday.—A verdict of "Accidentally drowned" was returned.

'A short time afterwards she struck on the sand. The sea swept over the deck and broke the bulwarks.'

'The vessel is now high and dry at low water.'

The bodies of Captain Guiseppe Matcovich and the boatswain, Teobila Svaglich, were found on Monday morning at Gunwalloe Cove. There was not a vestige of clothing on either body. An order for their burial was given by the coroner, no inquest being necessary in their case.

The crew of the Cviet were all Austrians, most of them big powerful men, in the prime of life. The survivors are greatly grieved at the loss of their shipmates, and are unanimous in the praise of their captain. One of the crew was very ill of fever and ague. Two or three of the others are suffering from scurvey, and the steward, the youngest of the crew, had a sprained ankle. In the hour of danger it was every one for himself. The strongest took the rope first to come ashore, and the poor fellow who had fever was last to get to dry land. He is now under the treatment of Mr. Rundle, surgeon, Porthleven, and is making rapid progress towards convalescence. The men are all staying at the Commercial Hotel, Porthleven, and are well cared for by Mr. and Mrs. Carah. Much has been said in favour of the noble conduct of the Porthleven fishermen, especially of Joseph Gilbert, who successfully threw the line on board, thus being the means of saving eight of the crew. At times, when he was going towards the ship, the waves took him off his legs, and for nearly a minute he would disappear beneath the seething waters, so that, at times, the bystanders thought he would be drowned. But, nothing daunted, when he came to the surface he persevered, and did not come back until he had effected a communication between the ship and the shore. It is believed he would have saved the life of the boatswain who made such a determined but unsuccessful struggle for life after he had lowered himself in the water, but Gilbert's two sons, who were holding the end of the rope which was around their father's waist, were afraid that if they allowed him more line he would be drowned. Gilbert's is, indeed, a case of bravery that deserves more than passing recognition. The coastguardsmen also deserve high commendation. Several of them rushed into the water and assisted the crew in landing. The vessel is now high and dry at low water, and it is considered that she is too far in to be broken up by the waves. She was built in Sunderland and launched in 1871.

(BY TELEGRAPH)

The funeral of the late captain, boatswain, and an able seaman, who lost their lives in the wreck of the Cviet, took place yesterday afternoon in Porthleven churchyard. The bodies had been placed in very neat coffins, and that of the captain was covered with the Austrian national flag.

'. . . and it is considered that she is too far in to be broken up by the waves.' Exceptionally, in this shipwreck some of the crew behaved badly. There was an unseemly scramble for safety. 'In the hour of danger it was every man for himself.'

The Suffolk

The Times, September 30, 1886

'No hope of saving the ship. She opened during the night through amidships five to six inches.'

THE SHIPWRECK AT THE LIZARD

———◆———

As was briefly announced in a telegram in *The Times* yesterday morning, the steamship Suffolk, of London, bound from Baltimore to London, with a general cargo and cattle, ran ashore close under the old Lizard Head at 10 minutes past 4 on Tuesday evening. The steamer, which is about 2,000 tons register, left Baltimore about a fortnight since, and all proceeded well until Sunday, when a lifeboat was carried away in a heavy sea. The Scilly Islands were sighted about 10 o'clock on Tuesday morning, but soon after this the weather became very thick and foggy. The steamer proceeded on her voyage, and all was thought to be well until suddenly, and without the slightest warning, the vessel struck the rocks. The crew at once realized their position, and the captain gave orders to have the boats lowered, and three were launched, into which the crew, of 41 hands, and two passengers were taken. The sea at the time was very heavy and was washing over the fore part of the vessel, where a portion of the cattle lay. The crew pulled seawards, as the night was intensely thick, and although soundings were taken they could only find that they were surrounded by rocks.

Meanwhile the disaster had been witnessed from the shore, and with great promptitude both the Cadgwith and Lizard lifeboats were launched and pulled to the scene. After much difficulty the three boats were fallen in with, but it was not until after the shipwrecked men had been knocking about for upwards of two hours in a heavy sea that the lifeboats succeeded in getting them safe on shore, and before that could be done two of the boats had to be abandoned and the occupants received into the lifeboats. It was expected that most of the cattle in the forepart of the vessel would be drowned. The Suffolk is owned by Messrs. Hooper, Murrell, and Co., of London.

Telegrams from Lloyd's signal station at the Lizard, received yesterday morning, state:—"Just returned from scene of wreck of the Suffolk; vessel still holding together, and some cattle are still alive, but sea too heavy to go near the ship. About 3,000 bags of flour have already been saved, having washed ashore. At high tide the spar deck was all awash. The captain and a portion of the crew have proceeded in Falmouth tugs to endeavour to save cattle, &c.; no hope of saving ship. Wind west, fresh; fog lifting.'' The Salvage Association, at the owners' request, have despatched a special officer to the wreck. The owners received the following telegram from the captain at midday yesterday:—"No hope of saving the ship. She opened during the night through amidships five to six inches. Cattle still standing on the after deck. The hulks and tugs lying off are waiting a chance to save them. A heavy surf is running, and the ship is full of water." A telegram received yesterday afternoon stated that the Suffolk was lying in the same position, and that a large rip was visible in the port side, just abaft the foremast, from which sacks of flour in great numbers were floating away. There is sand under her bows and stern, but the centre of the ship is firm on the rocks. The sea was moderating, and there was reason to hope that some of the cattle would be saved.

'It was expected that most of the cattle in the forepart of the vessel would be drowned.'

The Petrellen

Royal Cornwall Gazette, February 6, 1885

'But the Captain and crew persistently refused to leave the ship, notwithstanding the imminent peril in which she lay.'

THE GALE IN THE WEST.

WRECK IN MOUNT'S BAY

Early on Saturday morning the attention of the people in Penzance was directed to the perilous position of the Norwegian barque Petrellen, which was riding in the bay, of 340 tons register; she was in ballast homeward bound from Scotland. She proceeded up the Channel about a fortnight since as far as the Isle of Wight, but was driven back to Scilly by the strong easterly wind that then prevailed. She eventually fetched Mount's Bay and anchored there for shelter. The wind having changed from south to south-west, the master, Captain Knudsen, determined on Friday afternoon to make an attempt to get away. Owing however to the strong wind and the heavy sea it was found impossible to beat out the bay, and the Petrellen was brought up and anchored in the roads of St. Michael's Mount. Captain Knudsen subsequently went ashore at Penzance. As the night advanced the weather looked very threatening and the barometer fell rapidly, giving every indication of a dirty night. By many apprehensions were felt as to the safety of the barque, and more particularly was a fear entertained by Mr. A. Reed, the receiver of wreck, at whose thoughtful suggestion the lifeboat was brought round to the pier head as far back as Thursday, so that if her services should be required rescue might be expeditiously attempted. It was fortunate, as after events proved, that this suggestion was acted upon. In the early hours of Saturday morning the wind freshened considerably, and about 4 a.m. blew a stiff gale, with heavy squalls. The wind was then at south-south-west, veering to south-west, which naturally increased the violence of the sea. In porportion as this was seen to be the case fears deepened concerning the barque, on board of which, about 7 a.m. flambeaux were burnt to signal that she was in distress. The coastguard at Penzance promptly responded by throwing out rockets, and the lifeboat crew launched their boat with much smartness, and in a short time were making for the barque. By this time hundreds of people had assembled on the pier at Penzance and the scene was one of great animation. The progress of the lifeboat was watched with intense anxiety. The crew took with them Captain Knudsen, who had been in Penzance during the night, much to the general surprise. When the lifeboat reached the barque considerable relief was felt by the spectators and it was observed with satisfaction that she was able to bring the crew ashore and land them in safety. But the captain and mate persistently refused to leave the ship, notwithstanding the imminent peril in which she lay. The others of the crew were only too pleased to have an opportunity to leave her, being assured she would part, as her windlass was damaged. They were taken care of by the Norwegian vice-consuls, Messrs. W. D. Mathews and Sons. During Saturday the Petrellen remained in the Bay in much the same position as described, but the wind moder-

ated a good deal and the apprehension felt in regard to her was somewhat allayed.

On Sunday night the worst fears in regard to the barque were realised. The crew went on board in the morning and about six o'clock in the evening the captain resolved to make an effort to set sail. The wind was only blowing moderately at the time from the south-west. On getting up the cables one of them parted. Holding on by the other, which was the big chain, they got sail on the ship. They then began to get up the other anchor, but this cable also parted, and the barque driven back, went ashore on the Marazion beach, about a mile east of Penzance. The lifeboat, under the direction of the local secretary, Mr. Fred Mathews, was soon launched, and rescued the whole of the crew—ten in number. Captain Knudsen says the keel is knocked out of the barque. Captain Shirely, R.N., inspector of coastguard, was in attendance, as also were Mr. Reed, receiver of wreck, and Messrs. John and Edwin Mathews. The barque was partly owned by Captain Knudsen, and is now a total wreck.

'. . . and the lifeboat crew launched their boat
with much smartness.'

The **Castleford**

'All the crew are saved, but the vessel is a total wreck, and the greater part of the bullocks are drowned.'

The Cornishman, June 16, 1887

WRECK AT SCILLY.
460 BULLOCKS AND A CARGO OF WHEAT LOST.

The s.s. *Castleford*, Capt. McLean, from Montreal for London, having on board 460 head of cattle and a general cargo, ran on shore on Crebawethen (one of the Western Islands) on the evening of the 8th, at 7 p.m. A dense fog prevailed at the time. The *Castleford* was going full speed, struck hard, and remained immovable. The fore compartment was quickly full of water.

'Soon after striking, the chief officer and the boat's crew left the vessel to ascertain their position. The first thing they sighted was the Bishop's Light.' In 1887 the rebuilding of Bishop Rock Lighthouse was completed for the third time, and the light re-lit.

Soon after striking the chief officer and the boat's crew left the vessel to ascertain their position. The first thing they sighted was the Bishop light. Knowing their position they tried to get back; but, after long toiling, they found themselves back to the Bishop again.

They were now taken on board by a French fishing boat and remained till 3 a.m., when they left and landed at St. Mary's. The captain and crew did not leave the *Castleford* till daylight.

All the crew are saved, but the vessel is a total wreck, and the great part of the bullocks are drowned.

Nothing of the wreck was known at St. Mary's till 10.30 that night, when boats from St. Agnes and Bryher had returned from the scene of the disaster. The lifeboat was at once despatched.

The *Castleford* left Montreal on the 26th of May.

The *Castleford* still remains whole. About 60 head of cattle are saved and landed on Annet Island.

'The Castleford still remains whole.'

Penzance

The Malta

'The decks are all smashed in, the cargo is coming to the surface.'

Lake's Falmouth Packet and Cornwall Advertiser
October 19, 1889

Wreck of a Cunard Steamer.

Late on Tuesday evening the Cunard steamship "Malta," an iron screw steamship of 2,244 tons register, built at Glasgow in 1865, while proceeding from Liverpool to Falmouth, *en route* for the Mediterranean, ran ashore at Cape Cornwall, a very dangerous part of the coast. At the time the ship struck there was a dense fog, but otherwise the weather was fine. The captain and officers acted with much celerity and calmness, and thus prevented anything like a panic among the 18 passengers, every one of whom was landed safely. The work of rescuing the crew was then commenced, and they were all landed in perfect safety. Telegrams were at once sent to Messrs. G. C. Fox and Co. at Falmouth, the local agents of the company, who promptly sent two tugs to tow the "Malta" off, but they only succeeded in dragging her off the rocks, her stern settling down in deep water. The latest particulars to hand shew that she will very quickly become a total wreck. The decks are all smashed in, the cargo is coming to the surface, considerable wreckage is coming ashore, and salvors

'The cliff there is lofty and terribly steep.'

are busy all along the coast. The rock on which the "Malta" came to grief is not very far from the scene of the wreck of the "Asia" about two months ago. The cliff there is lofty and terribly steep, and the passengers could not possibly have got ashore had the sea been at all rough. None of the passengers' luggage was saved. One lady is said to have left £700 in a drawer on board, while others of the passengers had many valuables among their baggage.

On Wednesday a party of Sennen Cove fishermen put off to salve, securing a considerable quantity of goods, baggage, &c. On their return the sea struck the boat and turned it over, John Roberts, a fisherman of Sennen Cove, unfortunately being drowned. According to most accounts, when the Malta grounded, a scene of great confusion ensued, but only with the crew. Orders were given which were not obeyed; things that were required could not be found; and there was general disorder, arising probably from the fact that the crew were a scratch crew, and had had not many of them any previous knowledge of the vessel and the officers. An idea of the confusion which existed may be imagined from the fact that it

was an hour and three-quarters before the first boat was launched. Rockets were sent up from the ship as a signal to the coastguard, and some St. Just people who happened to be in the neighbourhood at the time quickly spread the news.

J.H. writing to the daily press says—"The matter ought not lightly to be passed over. The ship struck on a well-known rock, apparently through incompetency to take correct soundings. Even the passengers seem to have seen the land, which the look-out men failed to do. Who is responsible for sending this ship to sea with a 'scratch' crew, which surely means a crew of men totally unfit for their work? The Cunard have always been a company noted for the care they have taken to secure the safety of their passengers. If the account before us to-day be anywhere near the truth, the ship has been sacrificed, the passengers lives endangered, and their baggage lost, owing to the Malta having been sent to sea under conditions best calculated to bring about the disaster which followed."

The **Mohegan**

'Among traders there was an old-time saying: "Once inside the Manacles you will never get free again." '

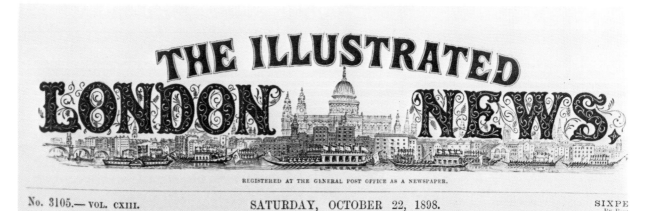

THE ILLUSTRATED LONDON NEWS

REGISTERED AT THE GENERAL POST OFFICE AS A NEWSPAPER.

No. 3105.—VOL. CXIII.   SATURDAY, OCTOBER 22, 1898.   SIXPE
By Post

Royal Cornwall Gazette, October 20, 1898

A LINER WRECKED ON THE MANACLES.

APPALLING LOSS OF LIFE.

TERRIBLE SCENES.

On Friday evening, in fairly good, clear weather, an appalling disaster occurred off the Cornish coast, where many a time before the blue waters from the Atlantic which roll down the mouth of the English Channel have swallowed up hundreds of human beings, and cast their whited corpses upon the rugged shore. About six or eight miles across the beautiful bay, west of Falmouth harbour, lie, as is well known to Cornish folk, the Manacle Rocks. Jutting out from the mainland topped by the spire of St. Keverne Church, is a beetling chain of treacherous rocks— treacherous, sharp, insidious. When weather is fair and light is clear, no mariner needs run his craft into the jaws of death which here may await him, for at all states of the tide one or more of the treacherous fangs rise gaunt and steep out of the waves. But in stress of weather, and in darksome nights, there is no light to warn him of his danger. South-westward are the Lizard lights, south-eastward the revolving light of St. Anthony. The only warning monitor that haunts the lonely, rockstrewn point is the solitary buoy which, swaying with the wind and tide, keeps up a perpetual tolling from its bell-top. Years has this warning voice sounded over the restless deep, many times has its message of mercy been turned into the death knell of scores of hapless men, women, and children as they struggled and fought for life where mercy had no ear. It was here on Friday evening that the liner Mohegan, of the Atlantic Transport Company, became a total wreck and caused the death of 97 lives.

The Late Captain Griffith

THE SCENE AT THE WRECK.

When the vessel struck there was at once a terrible rush for the deck by the panic-stricken passengers in the saloon; but neither the screams of the affrighted women and children, nor yet the obvious terrors of the situation appear to have unnerved the officers and crew for a moment. As one of the survivors, a horse shipper named George Maule, puts it, "The crew behaved like heroes. The captain stood on the bridge, and the greatest order prevailed among officers and crew." It was found that great holes had been torn in the ship on her starboard side forward, and that the

Where the Disaster Occurred

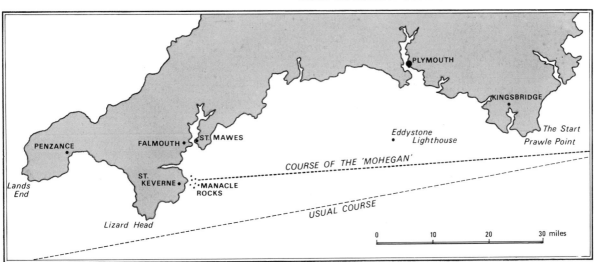

sea was pouring in through these holes in enormous quantities. She began to sink head first, and it was obvious she would not remain long above water. The electric lights were all extinguished, and darkness accentuated, if possible, the horrors of the situation. Women were passionately hugging their children and crying, "For God's sake, save us." In the midst of this heartrending scene there was heard the calm, stentorian words of Chief Officer Couch, "Now, boys, keep yourselves cool, and we will get the ladies and children off first." This sound, timely advice had a marvellous effect on the passengers. Most of them still wept bitterly, but they stood quiet, having implicit confidence that all would end well, because they saw the crew working so well in hand.

THE RECOVERY AND CARE OF THE DEAD

After the succouring of the living came the tender care and reverence for the dead. From daybreak onwards there were small parties of watchers looking out for the washing ashore around the coast of the bodies of the drowned. And they had not long to wait. From one point and another came only too frequently the story of "Another body picked up," and then there would be the gruesome task of removing the remains to places of temporary rest. The parish church of St. Keverne was the principal mortuary,

and by Saturday afternoon no less than fifteen bodies had been laid out in the south-east corner of the church, while other bodies had been reported as being lodged in farmhouses and other places within reach. But interest naturally centred chiefly in the church, and though the place was kept locked there were frequent visitors, mostly members of the crew who had been saved. There in the belfry, in the same corner (as the old lady who had charge of the place explained) were laid out 43 years ago the bodies of those lost by the wreck of the John, of whom 120 were buried in the adjoining yard, where also had been placed the remains of those thirteen men who perished in the Bay of Panama during the blizzard, and the five poor victims of the Annie Elizabeth—it was in the same place that this double row of corpses, which was being constantly added to, had been rested. They were in precisely the same condition as when picked up except that in each case the hands had been tied across the body.

PATHETIC SIGHTS AT IDENTIFICATION

It was a pathetic sight, and one which no one could witness without emotion, especially when the sheeting which had covered the features was cast aside and the face of a sweet little girl about twelve or thirteen, with pretty brown hair half shading her

'From one point and another came only too frequently the story of "another body picked up" and then there would be the gruesome task of removing the remains to places of temporary rest.'

'Women were passionately hugging their children and crying, "For God's sake save us." In the midst of this heartrending scene there was heard the calm stentorian words of Chief Officer Couch: "Now boys keep yourselves cool and we will get the ladies and children off first." . . . "All is over," cried Couch, for no sign of rescue was yet in sight, and stripping himself of everything but his underclothing he plunged overboard . . .'

The Late Llewelyn Couch, Chief Officer

forehead and falling down by the sides of her face, was revealed. The expression was suggestive of joy and rest, and as charming in death as it had been in life. On either side were tall women, one of whom had evidently received severe treatment against the rocks, for her face was covered with bruises and her clothes had been torn from her.

The Late Ernest Cole, Second Officer

A HEARTRENDING SCENE

Such demonstrations of the agony of human hearts in sore bereavement as have been witnessed within the walls of St. Keverne Church are happily rare. There was a most distressing incident on Tuesday morning. A poor woman dressed in black was in search of her dead husband, Robb, a steward. His body had been placed in a coffin, and the lid was removed as the woman was led weeping into the church. Directly she caught sight of the dead face she fell down and kissed it saying, " My God! and is he to be taken from me? How can I live alone?" For a long time she lovingly stroked the hands and kissed all over the face of her dead husband, and then, composing herself by a violent effort, got up and walked away. In a minute or so, however, she returned for one more inexpressibly sad and wistful gaze upon the dead, and then the coffin lid was fastened down. Scenes equally painful were enacted by the sides of other coffins. Under the superintendence of Mr. Orme Fox, a number of men were busily occupied all Tuesday morning in placing bodes in the plain stained wood coffins, which nearly covered the floor of the belfry end of the church.

THE GRAVES

From Sunday afternoon till Tuesday several men were engaged in digging a great grave within ten feet of the north wall of the church which faces Falmouth Bay. Night and day the gravediggers pushed their work, until on Tuesday morning a pit thirteen feet across, nineteen feet long, and ten feet deep, was excavated. It is situated in the older part of the churchyard, not twenty yards from the little headstone which records one of the most direful disasters which has ever happened, even on this fateful coast. This is the stone indicating the interment of one hundred and twenty persons drowned in the wreck of the John, in 1855. It was expected that about fourteen separate graves would be required, but on Tuesday morning only two were prepared, and these in the more modern section of the churchyard. This part, however, has but little room itself to spare. For the reception of the remains of young Marshall a grave was dug between two others, where there was barely room for it. Just over the pathway was the grave for another deceased passenger. Of the great common grave a plan has been prepared, on which will be shown the exact position of all the bodies buried in it, so that if it is desired to exhume any particular bodies at the request of those who have a right to claim them or erect headstones no difficulty will be found in locating them.

THE FUNERALS

There was a cessation on Tuesday of the deluge of rain, which had added so much to the misery of all engaged in the neighbourhood of the wreck, and the morning was colder and clearer. Gleams of sunshine gave a more genial aspect to sea and landscape, and although there was a little rain at the beginning of the funeral, the outdoor part of the rite was accomplished in fine weather. Precisely at 3 o'clock the church bell commenced to toll, and a congregation soon filled the church. The building has spacious aisles and plenty of vacant space at the belfry end, but all the accommodation was needed for the funeral service and the arrangement of the forty coffins containing the mortal remains of the victims. General identification having been practically completed, the bodies were set out in rows and numbered for placing in the grave according to the prepared plan. During the time the people were waiting for the commencement of the service the relatives of the deceased were naturally subject to much observation, and evidently regarded with whole-hearted sympathy. Some of the women, who had lost husbands, brothers, or sons, were broken down with grief, and all efforts to solace them were futile. One poor woman knelt on the stone floor, and alternately wrung her hands in despair, and rested on the coffin in the attitude of prayer, totally oblivious to all her surroundings. The survivors of the crew gathered in a little knot near the bodies of their lamented comrades and they could not conceal the emotion that possessed them.

GIBSON
Penzance
Copyright

The **Brinkburn**

The Cornishman, December 22, 1898

'A WRECK! A WRECK!'

WRECK OFF SCILLY.
Steamer Sunk, but Crew Saved.
(By telegraph from our own Correspondent.)

The steamer *Brinkburn*, of London, from Galveston for Havre, with 9000 bales of cotton and some cotton seed, ran on shore on the Maiden Bower, Isles of Scilly, about midnight, on Thursday, in a dense fog. The crew of 39 were all saved, but the ship will become a total wreck. Both lifeboats were soon on the spot, and the crew got into their own boats and were picked up by the Bryher boats.

SCILLONIAN DANCE INTERRUPTED BY WRECK.

On Thursday evening, Dec. 15th, the members of the Island-home tent I.O.R. had an at-home in the town hall, St. Mary's, Islands of Scilly, about 150 being present. The programme for the evening was:— Singing, music, and games from seven to nine. Then a cold collation of roast beef, ham, cake, and tea. After that the votaries of Terpsichore tripped the light fantastic toe. All went on as merrily as wedding-bells. There was no sound of revelry by night, as there was at Brussels on the night preceding the battle of Waterloo; but, just after midnight, while the strains of music still filled the hall and the merry dancers glided gracefully over the floor, each one intent on the movement of his or her partner, a shout rang through the hall

A WRECK! A WRECK!

In an instant, as if by magic, the scene was changed, and a general rush was made for the door—some to ascertain the accuracy of the news; others to proceed to the scene of the disaster, possibly of danger.

The Alarm Proved to be True;

for signal-guns and rockets had been heard and seen. In the meantime messages had been received from St. Agnes and Bryher establishing the fact. There was a dense fog at the time. The St. Mary's lifeboat was soon well on her way to the wreck. And

A Very Perilous Time They Had.

It was so dark that they could not see the length of the boat. The consequence was that they ran close to a ledge when three heavy swells broke so near them that every man clutched the life-lines.

When they got to the wreck they found it to be a large steamer—*Brinkburn*, of London, 2000 tons, Captain J. Martin, laden with cotton and cotton-seed, from Galveston for Havre.

The crew, 39 hands, many of whom were Lascars, had left in their own boats and were found by Bryher men. The vessel is on

The Maiden Bower Ledges,

and has become a total wreck. Several bales of cotton and bags of seed have been salved.

———

(Gathered by "The Cornishman's" Reporters on the Mainland.)

The dense fog of last week was the means of adding another to the enormous total of shipwrecks which the Scilly islands have witnessed. About midnight on Thursday signals of distress were heard at Bryher, and a crew soon manned a boat and went out to explore. After a time they fell in with a ship's gig, and soon after the other boats, of a big steamer which they found had struck on the Maiden Bower islet, about the westernmost island from Bryher. The islanders piloted the wrecked sailors to Bryher and there fed them, and clothed those of them who were wet through.

The steamer proved to be the *Brinkburn*, a London vessel, belonging to Messrs. Harris and Dickson, of London, commanded by Captain Martin. Her registered tonnage was 2096 tons, and she had on board a cargo which consisted of

9,000 Bales of Cotton, and About 300 Tons of Cotton-seed,

which she had been bringing from Galveston, Texas, U.S., for Havre. She ran into a thick fog when off Newfoundland five days before, and from that time until she was wrecked the fog never lifted. As the second watch were about to enter upon their duty, just before midnight on Thursday, the steamer ran over the ledge, and then crashed on to the Maiden Bower. The water at once

Rushed in so Furiously

that it was seen that something serious must have happened, and the captain at once ordered the boats to be manned and the crew promptly launched them and stood by the sinking ship. But their signals had been heard and the Bryher boat came on the scene and piloted them into Bryher.

Kindness of Bryher Folk.

Here they were most hospitably received, fires having been prepared by the inhabitants, and refreshment and sleeping accommodation being at once provided for the men, who numbered 39, and were composed of 22 Lascars, and nine Englishmen, while the remainder were Swedes, Norwegians, Russians, and Italians. About seven on the next morning, Friday, it was seen that

The Vessel had Nearly Disappeared ;

but a small part of the bow was observable, the hull being very badly torn with a huge rent.

The crew were unable to save even their clothing, and their wants in this respect were attended to by Mr. Gibson, the agent for the Shipwrecked mariners' society, who had to provide the Lascars with entirely new things, as they were only clothed, when they escaped, in their usual working costume of calico. On Friday more clothing was sent for the men from Penzance to Mr. Gibson.

The Shipwrecked Crew

were brought to Penzance on Monday by the *Lyonnese*, and were at once received by Messrs. Mathews, Lloyds' agents, and most of them left on the following day for their respective homes. As an instance of

The Density of the Fog

it may be mentioned that during thick fogs gun-cotton bombs are exploded at intervals from the lighthouse on Bishop's-rock, but though the *Brinkburn* passed within seven miles, at which distance they are usually easily heard, nothing was heard by her. While the St. Mary's lifeboat could not hear the bombs from three miles off, though the signals of the distressed vessel were distinguishable. If the sea had been rough there would have been but a faint chance of any of the sailors being saved ; for, than among Scilly's rocks and ledges in darkness and unpiloted, there are

Few More Dangerous Places.

About 100 bales of cotton had been saved up to Sunday out of the 9000.

The s.s. *Hyena*, on behalf of Lloyd's, left Liverpool on Saturday for Scilly to carry out salving operations. She was expected at Scilly on Monday.

Narrative of the Man at the Wheel.

The helmsman at the time the *Brinkburn* struck, said that the steamer, which was of 2,056 tons register, was 16 days out from Newport-News, being bound from Galveston to Havre with a comparatively light cargo, comprising 9,000 bales of cotton and 30,000 bags of cottonseed. The vessel's crew, which numbered 39, was composed, for the most part, of Hindoo Coolies and Lascars from South America, the remainder being English, Swedes, and Italians. The Darkies were principally employed in the stoke-holes. Four days before the catastrophe the *Brinkburn* ran into

An Exceedingly Thick Fog.

The steamer's speed was not lessened : she was kept at full speed all the time : and she struck the rocks head on about a quarter to twelve, the shock being tremendous. She ran right on a ledge of rock, and the heavy sea which prevailed at the time made movements on board somewhat difficult and dangerous. The captain ordered

The Ship's Boats, Four in Number, to be Lowered,

and when this was done the crew were instructed to save their lives by leaving the vessel, which by this time had been gradually gliding off the rocks, this caused by the tremendous power and rush of the huge waves as they leapt at the doomed ship and over the jagged rocks. At first the captain demurred to leaving his charge, but, on seeing how matters stood, he wisely decided that it was better to abandon the steamer and see to the safety of the many lives entrusted to his care. The boats left the steamer about half-past one, just as

The "Brinkburn" Sank in Deep Water,

and shortly afterwards they landed on one of the group of the Scilly islands.

'About 100 bales of cotton had been saved up to Sunday out of the 9,000.'

The Seine

The Cornishman, January 3, 1901

A DISASTROUS DECEMBER GALE.
GREAT LOSS OF LIFE
BRAVERY AND EXCITING SCENES.

What has been described as probably the worst gale experienced for the last 20 years broke over the United Kingdom on Thursday night, and caused many wrecks and a great loss of life round the coast. Cornwall had its share of catastrophes, there being a number of disasters on its coast. Now for details.

BARQUE GOES TO PIECES AT PERRANPORTH.

RESCUE OF 24 LIVES

On Friday an exciting scene was witnessed at Perranporth. Soon after 10 o'clock the coastguards at St. Agnes observed a large sailing vessel in difficulties. All her sails were blown away with the exception of the two foretopsails, which were in ribbons. After a desperate attempt to tack up along the coast the vessel ran before the gale and, eventually, grounded on the soft sand at Perran. The St. Agnes rocket brigade, after nine futile attempts to establish communication with the vessel, succeeded in sending a rocket on board. Exciting scenes followed, the crew being pulled through the boiling surf in an exhausted condition. When half the crew had been rescued the rocket apparatus broke and the remainder lowered themselves by ropes in the five feet of water at the ship's side and were assisted ashore by ready helpers, prominent among whom were Messrs. D. Hounsell and P. Higgins. Ultimately the whole of the ship's company were safely landed and hospitably treated.

The stranded vessel proved to be the iron barque *Seine,* of Dunkerque, which left Iquique on Sep. 25th with a cargo of saltpetre for Falmouth. The voyage had lasted over 90 days, and during the last ten heavy weather, with constantly shifting wind, had been experienced. During Friday night the barque became a total wreck, the beach at Perranporth being strewn with wreckage.

'During Friday night the barque became a total wreck, the beach of Perranporth being strewn with wreckage.'

The King Cadwallon

The Cornishman, July 26, 1906

'Several boats arrived from the different Islands and offered to salve all the light gear about the deck . . . but their offer of assistance was refused, the Captain evidently preferring that everything should go with the ship.'

STEAMER ASHORE AT SCILLY

The steamship King Cadwallon, 2,126 tons register, from Barry for Naples, struck an outlying rock off the Scillies, called Hard Lewis, during a dense fog at five o'clock on Sunday morning. A farmer at St. Elbary's, named Owen Legg, heard the vessel's signals of distress, and with his sons put to sea in a small boat, and ascertained the whereabouts of the King Cadwallon. She had her fore compartment full of water, but the crew stood by their ship. The captain wired to Falmouth for a tug, which left for the

wreck. Locally it is considered improbable that the ship can be refloated. The sea is calm. The King Cadwallon belongs to the King Line, Limited, of Glasgow.

Our St. Mary's correspondent writes:—The s.s. King Cadwallon from Barry, bound to Naples went ashore on the Hard Lewis Rocks, near St. Martin's Head, about half past five on Sunday morning. Rockets were fired as soon as she struck, and were heard by Mr. Williams, of Borough, St. Mary's, and Mr. Owen Legg, of Watermill. They and their sons

THE CORNISHMAN:

went off to the wreck and brought the captain ashore to St. Mary's to report his ship ashore and to telegraph for a salvage steamer. Meanwhile the crew got out the ship's boats, and having provisioned them, left the ship, and lay off in their boats, fearing that the ship which had a heavy list to starboard, might fall off in deep water. Several boats arrived from the different Islands and offered to salve all the light gear about the deck and also the ship's stores, but their offer of assistance was refused, the captain evidently preferring that everything should go with the ship. The only things removed from the ship were the stores which were subject to duty and these the Custom officers had taken on shore. In the afternoon when the tide flowed the vessel was almost submerged, just the bulwarks on the port side being above water. The crew numbering 26 were landed at St. Mary's in the afternoon.

On Monday morning the Lady of the Isles arrived and went out to the wreck, when the tide was low. Capt. Anderson brought ashore two of the boats which had been left in the davits, one of the boats being damaged by the sea during the night. There is not much prospect of saving any quantity of materials from the ship, all her cabins and engine room being full of water, and her cargo of coal is not likely to pay to work out.

———

Several members of the crew of the King Cadwallon arrived at Penzance on Monday evening and proceeded to their respective homes.

'In the afternoon when the tide flowed, the vessel was almost submerged, just the bulwarks on the port side being above water.'

The **Khyber**

'The terrible fury of the wind drove the waves clean over the ship.'

The Royal Cornwall Gazette

FALMOUTH PACKET, CORNISH WEEKLY NEWS AND GENERAL ADVERTISER.

Royal Cornwall Gazette, March 16, 1905

TERRIBLE SHIPPING CALAMITY
OFF THE LAND'S END

TWENTY-THREE LIVES LOST.

The British ship Khyber foundered near the Land's End yesterday, when twenty-three persons were drowned and three were saved. The Khyber was an iron ship, and was homeward bound from Melbourne. She was a sailing ship of 2,026 tons gross, built in 1880, and was owned by the Galgate Shipping Co., Ltd., of Liverpool. The ship's voyage was a pleasant one till several days ago, when severe weather was encountered. Later the sails were blown away, and the ship became unmanageable. The crew were then able to make out the Lizard light to the south'ard, and fired rockets and made signals of distress. All day on Tuesday the ship was blown before the gale, and as night came on they found they were on a leeshore, and slowly being blown on the coast. No more signals of distress were left, and apparently the vessel was not observed on shore. Just outside the Millbay Creek, between the Runnelstone and the Land's End, the crew let go two anchors at 11 o'clock on Tuesday night, and the Khyber lay, bow out to sea, not more than 400 yards away from the mainland. The terrible fury of the wind drove the waves clean over the ship. Each time she sank in the trough of the sea she was submerged from stem to stern. For seven long hours the crew had been clinging to the rigging, their only place of refuge, when slowly but surely the vessel began to drift on the rocks, and just before seven o'clock the Khyber struck astern. Her bow was forced round, bringing her broadside on to the waves. In ten minutes she was a total wreck. Nothing could be seen of her but broken wood and pieces of timber thrown around the cove. Most of the crew had left the vessel, but ere the cables parted, or the anchors were dragged,

'In ten minutes she was a total wreck. Nothing could be seen of her but broken wood and pieces of timber thrown around the cove.'

the mizzen mast went by the board, and the five men clinging to it were thrown into the sea. They made a gallant but unavailing struggle for life, and quickly disappeared from the sight of those who, on shore, were watching the catastrophe in helpless inactivity. Some of the crew jumped into the sea, but only three managed to reach land.

A young lad named Willis, of Liverpool, was washed ashore with some wreckage. Fortunately Mr John E. Soloman, of Plymouth, was able to render first aid, and after persevering three-quarters of an hour, Willis recovered. The other two survivors were thrown by the waves against a rock which juts out of the sea. They clambered up, both having reached it by means of wreckage, to which they clung.

'A young lad named Willis of Liverpool was washed ashore with some wreckage. Fortunately Mr. John E. Soloman of Plymouth was able to render first-aid, and after persevering three-quarters of an hour Willis recovered.'

52

The **T. W. Lawson**

'She only struck once more, and then came destruction. Masts and rigging crashed into the sea and the stern was cut right off.'

Lake's Falmouth Packet, Cornwall Advertiser, and Visitors' List, December 20, 1907

Terrible Wreck off Scilly.

Seventeen Men Drowned.

The wreck of a huge American sailing ship at the Isles of Scilly, involving the loss of many lives, early on Saturday morning, augments the dreadful roll the islands have claimed. The story of how the largest sailing ship in the world was cut in twain among the rocks reveals a harrowing story of fate of those who went down with the Thomas W. Lawson, and of the three men who survived her until Sunday when one of those failed to escape death. The doomed vessel was seven-masted and schooner rigged, and the largest sailing ship afloat. She belonged to Boston, Mass., U.S.A., and was built five years ago, of steel, and was constructed especially to save labour in crew. She only carried a captain and crew of seventeen. Captain Geo. W. Dow, of Boston, was her master, and she sailed from Philadelphia on November 20th last. The ship was valued at 100,000 dollars, and her cargo was worth approximately 200,000 dollars. The cargo consisted of oil, and it is computed that in bulk there were about 60,000 barrels. The net tonnage was about 5,000 tons. From the start the vessel had a bad passage.

On Friday last the vessel made the Isles of Scilly, and the captain found he was too far to the leeward by a mile. There was no room to wear ship and there was not sail enough to tack. The ship was, therefore, brought to and anchored. Her position was dangerous. She was in waters teeming with rocks and submerged ledges, between Nun Deeps and Gunner's Ledges and in Broad Sound. This is inside Bishop Lighthouse, which was first reported on the ship as a passing schooner. The Thomas W. Lawson, with two anchors out, faced the fury of a fierce north-west gale. Accompanying the gale were mountainous seas, and the ship could not have been in a worse position. She had been sighted from St. Agnes and St. Mary's Islands, and realizing her extreme danger, the St. Agnes lifeboat was launched. The keepers on the lighthouse also saw her and fired signals. St. Mary's lifeboat was being manned and launched at 4.26 by order of Mr. E. J. Bluett, hon. secretary of the local branches of the Lifeboat Institution. Both lifeboats had trying experiences, as seas continually broke over them. The St. Agnes boat was launched about four o'clock, and reached the ship shortly after five. The captain was asked if he wanted assistance, and replied in the negative. Knowing the danger in which the vessel stood, the lifeboatmen again asked, and got alongside. Captain Dow then requested the services of a pilot. One of the lifeboat crew, William Cook Hicks, a well-known Trinity pilot, went aboard, but all that could be done was to wait for moderation of weather. The lifeboat stood by the ship. St. Mary's lifeboat afterwards arrived, and in attempting to get alongside got under the quarter of the vessel and carried away her mast. She returned to St. Mary's to repair the damage and to send telegrams to Falmouth for tugs. The reply from Falmouth was that the tugs left at 10.20 on Friday night. The tugs never arrived, evidently finding the gale too fierce to face. The St. Agnes boat had to leave the ship in order to take ashore one of their crew, who had suffered from exposure. It was feared he was dead, but restoration was brought about when he was taken ashore. Hicks, the pilot on board, was informed, and told that should anything untoward happen he was to burn flares. Neither of the lifeboats went back. A sharp lookout was kept from various points. At 2.30 on Saturday morning the ship's lights disappeared. As the gale had heightened, it was thought at St. Agnes that the lights had been accidentally extinguished. Little did the watchers realise that the Thomas Lawson had gone to her doom, and that of the nineteen souls aboard, including one of their own mates, only three were at that time struggling from death to tell the tale of the tragic fate of the ship.

The Thomas Lawson broke an anchor unable to stand the hurricane, and, dragging the other, crashed into the rocks. The officers and pilot were in the mizzen-rigging, lashed, between two and three o'clock, and the remainder were scattered in different parts of the ship, the chief on the forecastle head. The ship struck broadside on, smashing in the starboard side, and causing rigging to sag until the seven masts began to sway with the motion of the vessel as she was buffeted by huge seas. It was a desperate and awful time. The engineer, Edward Rowe, of Boston, was by the side of the pilot, and when the huge craft trembled from end to end as she was hurled against the rocks, he asked Hicks if there was a chance of getting ashore. Hicks knew every inch of that treacherous part, and replied: "No." But strangely enough, that engineer is one of the survivors. Hicks, to the regret of all Scillonians, is missing, and is undoubtedly dead. The end of the ship came swiftly. She only struck once more, and then came destruction. Masts and rigging crashed into the sea and the stern was cut right off. The cargo was freed, and thousands of gallons of oil poured out on to the sea. Every man had a lifebelt, but nearly all were either dragged down in the rigging, dashed against rocks, or perished in the horrible floating masses of oil.

Out of the vortex came Captain Dow, the engineer, and George Allen, of Battersea. They had terrible hardships to pass through before finding a refuge on the rocks. Terrible privations followed in full exposure to the awful weather. For many hours those on the islands were still watching, ignorant of what had happened. Daybreak revealed no ship, but the most overwhelming stench of oil told its own story. The lifeboat was not launched, the weather being too fearfully rough, and it was not thought advisable even to try to get her out at St. Agnes. The grown-up son of pilot Hicks pleaded for an endeavour to launch the lifeboat when the lights of the ship disappeared. At daybreak a crew volunteered to go out with a gig, and eight young St. Agnes men including pilot Hicks's son, heroically launched it. They landed on the uninhabited island of Annet, and then heard the faint shouting for help. A search revealed the sailor Allen suffering from exposure and internal injuries trying to get shelter beneath a rock. He had been weathering the storm on the same shore as three of his mates, but they were dead. He saw them at daybreak, and evidently there was life in them then. He urged his rescuers to go to them, as he was all right. Allen was borne to St. Agnes Island and placed under the roof of a hospitable farmer, Mr. Israel Hicks. Communication was set up with St. Mary's, and St. Mary's lifeboat took Dr. Brashfield to St. Agnes, and he attended the injured man. The doctor did not regard his recovery with any hopes. Allen was then apparently the sole survivor, and he had been taken from an island two miles from where the vessel had anchored and was left by lifeboats. Allen had been on the island about five hours, and was the last man washed off the vessel. The islanders almost gave up hope that any other man could be living on the rocks in the vicinity.

The same crew, however, made another brave row to Annet Island, leaving St. Agnes about 2.30 Saturday afternoon, and they were rewarded by finding a

HAVOC OF THE GALE: FLOODS, AND AN EXTRAORDINARY WRECK.

1. THE ST. AGNES LIFE-BOAT, WHICH PUT HICKS (X) ON BOARD.
2. WILLIAM C. HICKS, TRINITY PILOT, DROWNED AT THE WRECK.
3. WORKED BY NINETEEN MEN: THE WONDERFUL SAILING-VESSEL.
4. THE SCENE OF THE WRECK (X), THE WESTWARD ROCKS, SCILLY.

THE LOSS OF THE WORLD'S GREATEST SAILING-VESSEL: THE SEVEN-MASTED SCHOONER "THOMAS W. LAWSON."

Shortly before dark on the evening of December 13 the "Thomas W. Lawson," the largest sailing-vessel in the world, bound from Philadelphia to London, anchored between the Island of St. Mary and the Bishop Lighthouse, Scilly. The St. Agnes life-boat put the Trinity pilot Hicks on board, and it was hoped that the vessel would ride out the storm. Next morning, however, she struck and turned turtle. Of her crew

STATISTICS OF THE "THOMAS W. LAWSON."	
Tonnage	4914 tons.
Length	375 feet.
Spread of Canvas	43,000 feet.
Weight of Sails	18 tons.
Crew	19 men.

of nineteen men three only were rescued. One of the three died after he was brought ashore. Hicks, the pilot, was also drowned. The "Thomas W. Lawson" was of 4914 tons. She was built five years ago at Quincy, Massachusetts. All her rigging was worked by steam-winches, and in spite of her vast sail area a crew of nineteen could work her perfectly.—[PHOTOGRAPHS NOS. 1, 3, AND 4 BY GIBSON.]

Illustrated London News, December 21, 1907

man safe and well. On their way they saw the engineer on a rock at Helwethers Carn. They threw him a rope, and with its aid he got through the surf and into the boat. Rowe then told them that the captain was on the rocks there helpless. How he got there he did not know, but he discovered him in the night and dragged him up into comparative safety. Rowe himself was badly battered, and suffering through swallowing salt water and oil. They took him ashore and went back to rescue the captain. Captain Dow undoubtedly owes his life to Fred Cook Hicks, a son of Pilot Hicks, who has not been found. They could not effect a landing, and Hicks thereupon took the rope and swam and scrambled through nearly fifty yards of sea and rocks. His difficulties were not then over, as he found the captain helpless with wounds he had received through being tossed about and with a broken wrist. Hicks

securely fastened him with a rope and managed to get him to the gig. Captain Dow was taken to the same house in which Allen and Rowe were sheltered, and was attended, Dr. Brushfield being again taken out by the St. Mary's lifeboat, and the lifeboatmen searched the rocks to try and trace other men of the ship.

Allen died on Sunday afternoon, so that the only survivors are the captain and the engineer. It is understood that the ship is not insured.

Up to Monday five bodies were recovered. The vessel has become a hopeless wreck and her fourteen tanks, containing 6,000 gallons of oil, have emptied themselves into the sea.

At the inquest on victims of the disaster, verdicts of "Accidental death" were returned, and the jury recommended that the two lifeboat stations should work together in a greater measure than at present.

The **Plympton**

'When the ship turned turtle and foundered
there were nine or ten men aboard, three of
them being visitors to the Island.'

'A number of boats were alongside the vessel,
loading cargo at the time, and had a narrow
escape.'

Lake's Falmouth Packet, Cornwall Advertiser, and Visitors' List, August 20, 1909

SCILLY DISASTER.

Ship on Rocks Sinks During Salvage Operations.

Two Islanders Drowned.

Sailed from Falmouth.

Within a few hours of sailing from Falmouth on Friday the steamer Plympton, of London, went ashore during a thick fog at St. Agnes, Scilly. The Plympton arrived at Falmouth last week with a cargo of maize from Rosario for orders. She anchored off St. Anthony lighthouse and left on Friday for Dublin.

Dense fog prevailed in the vicinity of the Scilly Isles throughout Friday and on Saturday morning. Throughout Friday night steamers' hooters were sounded in all directions, and on Saturday morning the Plympton, went ashore on a ledge on the south side of St. Agnes, called Lethegus. A coastguard at St. Agnes saw the vessel and communicated with St. Mary's, and the lifeboat was launched. Many boats from St. Agnes and St. Mary's also put to sea in search of the vessel, it being at the time impossible to see more than a few yards. With rocks above and below water in all directions, this was very dangerous work, but the ship was ultimately found and large quantities of her cargo of Indian corn were brought to St. Mary's where it was stored.

From the position in which the Plympton lay on the ledge it was felt during the day that there was little doubt but that she would become a total wreck, though there was no danger to her crew, as the sea was perfectly calm. This fear as to the fate of the vessel was justified during Saturday afternoon, when she suddenly turned over and went down, only the bow being visible.

When the ship turned turtle and foundered there were nine or ten men on board, three of them being visitors to the Islands, who had gone with the boatmen from St. Mary's to see the wreck. Two islanders—Charles Mumford, of St. Mary's, and Charles Hicks, of St. Agnes—were drowned.

Visitor's Remarkable Escape.

One of the visitors who had a very fortunate escape, was Mr. Ormrod, who has for many years spent most of the summer cruising among the islands. He was in the deck house when the rush of water nearly overpowered him. He managed to get through the door, rose to the surface and was picked up. He injured his hand getting clear of the door. Most of the others managed to reach the weather rail and jumped, but Mumford and Hicks were not seen again. It is thought that they must have got entangled in some of the gear. Mumford leaves a wife and one child.

A number of boats were alongside the vessel loading cargo at the time and had a narrow escape. The men who escaped from the wreck had to swim for their lives and were picked up by the boats. The crew of the Plympton were taken to St. Mary's on Saturday evening, and were taken charge of by Mr. J. C. Rogers, agent of the Shipwrecked Mariners' Society.

The thick fog continued all day on Saturday, and the Lyonesse, from Penzance, with a large number of passengers on board, had a very narrow escape in making the islands. She was unable to make the return journey on Saturday, the captain deeming it advisable to wait till Sunday morning.

Another correspondent says the steamer was on a voyage from Rosario to Dublin, with maize, and had put into Falmouth for orders. The crew numbered 23, and the chief officer's wife was on board. When the vessel turned over and sank, four men who were in the cabin at the time had a very narrow escape. Messrs. Mumford and Hicks were either in the cabin or hold of the steamer, and were carried down with her.

Had the accident happened a few minutes later more lives would have been lost, as several boats had just arrived at the wreck, and their crews would have been in the hold salving the cargo.

The Plympton was a steel steamer of 2,869 tons, built in 1893 by Furness, Withy and Co., and owned by Lambert Bros. (Limited), London. Her voyage was from the Plate to the United Kingdom or Continent, had to call at Falmouth for orders, and was bound for Dublin to discharge. Her hull is valued at £16,000, and her maize cargo at £25,000, both covered in London. In shipping disasters it is curious how one casualty in the same ownership is often quickly followed by another. The Plympton is the second boat of Lambert Bros. to be in trouble in a few days, the other being the Manaton ashore, but floated off the Smalls. The position of the Plympton is bad, and underwriters have paid 70 guineas to reinsure.

No further salvage has been possible in the wrecked steamer Plympton. The after part of the vessel has gone down in 15 fathoms of water, and the bow is sticking up perpendicularly, with a strong list, too dangerous to work on. The bodies of the two islanders drowned have not yet been recovered and have probably been swept away by the strong spring tides now running. On Sunday afternoon the Rev. R. A. Bosanquet, chaplain of the Isles, visited the wreck, and read the Burial Service on board.

'The after part of the vessel has gone down in
15 fathoms of water and the bow is sticking up
perpendicularly with a strong list too
dangerous to work on.'

The City of Cardiff

Lake's Falmouth Packet, Cornwall Advertiser, and Visitors' List, March 29, 1912

Cornish Coast Wreck.

Splendid Life-Saving Work by Sennen Brigade.

25 Persons Landed.

The City of Cardiff, a steamer only six years old, commanded by Capt. Story, was driven ashore on the Cornish Coast, not far from Land's End, yesterday week. It followed on a succession of wrecks on or off the Cornish coast which makes the past winter unprecedented in the toll it has taken of shipping. Happily, the loss of life has been very small. In this case there was none, and, in saving 26 lives, the crew of the Sennen life-saving apparatus performed another act of splendid service. The City of Cardiff went ashore only half a mile away from where the steamer Winborne was smashed up on the rocks in a gale in November, 1910, when just in the nick of time the same life-saving crew took off from her by means of the apparatus 27 persons.

The City of Cardiff was the second Welsh steamer wrecked on the rock-bound coast of Cornwall in the vicinity of Land's End within seven days, the steamer South America going ashore only a little way further up the coast, where she has remained fast. Mill Bay, where the City of Cardiff came to destruction, is an inlet to the eastward of Land's End, and forms part of an awful coast. It is the cove where the only survivor of the ill-fated Spanish ship Febrero was washed ashore in February, 1910. The City of Cardiff was in ballast, and bound for Cardiff from Havre, where she had discharged. She failed to enter the Bristol Channel yesterday week, when a moderate gale, about west by north, of 6 to 8 force, blew, afterwards freshening.

Vigilant Look-out.

The saving of all hands was primarily due to the vigilant look-out kept by the coastguard at Tol-pedn-Penwith and by the bad weather observer at Land's End, for from beginning to end no signal of distress was displayed by the steamer. The action of the coastguard and the life-saving apparatus crew was most prompt and timely, as tremendous seas swept over the ship and began to rend her. She was observed to be in difficulties about eleven o'clock in the morning, the vessel being light, and apparently unable to face the

'A tremendous sea swept over the ship and began to rend her.'

gale. Later, information reached Lieut. Chambers, of Penzance, the divisional commander of coastguards, that a steamer was in distress about a mile from Tol-Pedn, where the captain had had to heave-to. He had both his anchors in the hope of riding out the gale, and was keeping his engine at full steam ahead to ease his cable and hold off from the shore. Arriving in his motor car, Lieut. Chambers found that the vessel was a mile and a half southward of Land's End, and only half a mile from the shore on the southern side of Mill Bay. For a long time the captain kept his engine going at full steam. Meanwhile, the Sennen life-saving apparatus, in charge of Chief Officer Rees, had been summoned, and the Tol-Pedn cliff ladder, in charge of Chief Petty Officer Halkins, sent for. The Sennen lifeboat was called out, but, although launched, could not get out in the face of the heavy seas.

As no horses were available, the life-saving apparatus wagon was dragged by the crew some three miles and when some horses were procured, and Tol-Pedn reached, considerable difficulty still faced the crew, and the gear had to be carried for a considerable distance over a rough country. Meanwhile the weather had freshened, and the sea and wind made the ship drag her anchors slowly towards the shore for about 50 yards. In one final and desperate effort to save his ship the captain weighed one of his anchors, steaming hard the whole time; but a tremendous squall swept down, turning the ship broadside on and driving her rapidly ashore. In turn the captain paid the cable out again, in the hope that the anchor would hold, but the wind shifted two points to the south, and brought the vessel away to the northward a little. The gale then caught her on the starboard beam, and that was the beginning of the end. One of the cables parted, and it was obvious to those on shore that nothing could save the vessel, and steps were taken to endeavour to save those on board.

The vessel came in bow on, but soon swung round to the sea broadside on, and she struck about 150 yards out from the rocks which rise rather precipitously. Owing to the steepness of the cliffs the tripod of the life-saving apparatus could not be used. The first rocket fell short. The second was fired by Lieut. Chambers and hit the foot of the City of Cardiff's mast. The whip was secured by those on board, and a hawser was then sent out and made fast. The hawser was secured on shore by fastening it around a large rock, the pinnacle of a cluster about 80 feet above the sea. In addition to the captain and the 22 hands on board were the captain's wife and the chief officer's wife and child, a boy about five years of age. Life-belts were served out to all of them.

There was much excitement when the breeches buoy was sent out to the wreck, and the first person to be hauled ashore was the captain's wife. Then came the chief officer's wife, and she was followed by a member of the crew with the chief officer's child. One by one the remainder of the hands were brought ashore, most of them with some of their personal belongings. The ship's papers, cashbox, and other articles were secured. The captain was the last to leave the ship. Perfect discipline prevailed aboard the ship, and all hands were quite calm and collected. The captain had a most trying experience, for he was on the bridge for over twelve hours. The crew were taken charge of by Mr. Matthews, agent for the Shipwrecked Mariners' Society. and conveyed to Land's End. Late on Thursday night they were taken to Penzance.

When the vessel struck on a sandbank it was about $5\frac{1}{2}$ hours' ebb, and with the rising tide and gale she was carried right on to the rocks within 60 yards of the shore. There was absolutely no chance for the ship, the sea sweeping over her furiously, pounding the steamer on the rocks until her plates began to open and her decks cleared of the fittings until the waters around were a mass of broken wreckage. In a few hours she was a total wreck.

_____

'. . . the crew of the Sennen life-saving
apparatus performed another act of splendid
service.'

(Over) Relief of Bishop Light, 1977, by Frank Gibson.